American & European Art

Featuring: Property from the Lucien Abrams Collection • Property from The Houston Club
Property from a Texas Private Collection

November 8, 2011 | Dallas

LIVE AUCTION Signature® Floor Sessions

(Floor, Telephone, HERITAGE Live!,™ Internet, Fax, Mail)

Heritage Auctions Design District Annex
1518 Slocum Street • Dallas, TX 75207

Tuesday, November 8 • 10:00 AM CT • Lots 64001–64152

LOT SETTLEMENT AND PICK-UP

Available immediately following session or weekdays
9:00 AM - 5:00 PM CT by appointment only

Lots are sold at an approximate rate of 75 lots per hour, but it
is not uncommon to sell 60 lots or 100 lots in any given hour.

This auction is subject to a 19.5% Buyer's Premium.

TX Auctioneer licenses: Robert Korver 13754; Scott Peterson 13256; Bob Merrill 13408; Mike
Sadler 16129; Andrea Voss 16406; Jacob Walker 16413; Eric Thomas 16421; Marsha Dixey
16493; Tim Rigdon 16519; Cori Mikeals 16582; Stewart Huckaby 16590; Chris Dykstra 16601;
Teia Baber 16624; Peter Wiggins 16635. Associates under sponsorship of Tim Rigdon 16519:
Ed Beardsley 16632.

PRELIMINARY LOT VIEWING Select Highlights

Heritage Auctions, New York
445 Park Avenue • New York, NY 10022

Thursday, October 20 – Wednesday, October 26
10:00 – 6:00 PM ET

LOT VIEWING

Heritage Auctions Design District Annex
1518 Slocum Street • Dallas, TX 75207

Thursday, November 3 – Saturday, November 5
10:00 AM – 5:00 PM CT
Sunday, November 6 • 12:00PM – 4:00 PM CT
Monday, November 7 • 9:00 AM – 5:00 PM CT

View lots & auction results online at HA.com/5069

BIDDING METHODS:

HERITAGE Live!™ Bidding
Bid live on your computer or mobile, anywhere in the world,
during the Auction using our HERITAGE Live!™ program at
HA.com/Live

Live Floor Bidding
Bid in person during the floor sessions.

Live Telephone Bidding (floor sessions only)
Phone bidding must be arranged on or before Monday,
November 7, by 12:00 PM CT. Client Service: 866-835-3243.

Internet Bidding
Internet absentee bidding ends at 10:00 PM CT
the evening before each session. HA.com/5069

Fax Bidding
Fax bids must be received on or before Monday, November 7,
by 12:00 PM CT. Fax: 214-409-1425

Mail Bidding
Mail bids must be received on or before Monday, November 7.

Phone: 214-528-3500 • 800-872-6467
Fax: 214-409-1425
Direct Client Service Line: 866-835-3243
Email: Bid@HA.com

This Auction is presented and cataloged by Heritage Auctions
© 2011 Heritage Auctioneers & Galleries, Inc.

HERITAGE HA.com
AUCTIONS

25539

Fine & Decorative Arts Specialists

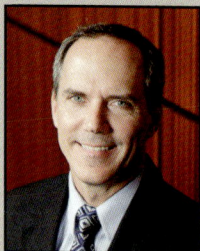

Steve Ivy
CEO
Co-Chairman of the Board

Jim Halperin
Co-Chairman of the Board

Greg Rohan
President

Paul Minshull
Chief Operating Officer

Todd Imhof
Executive Vice President

Ed Beardsley
Vice President and
Managing Director,
Fine and Decorative Arts

Ed Jaster
Sr. Vice President

Ariana Hartsock
Consignment Director

Marianne Berardi, Ph.D.
Senior Fine Arts Expert

Kirsty Buchanan
Consignment Director

3500 Maple Avenue • Dallas, Texas 75219
Phone 214-528-3500 • 800-872-6467
HA.com/FineArt

Consignment Directors: Ariana Hartsock, Marianne Berardi Ph.D.,
Ed Jaster, Ed Beardsley, Kirsty Buchanan
Cataloged by: Laura Howard, Marianne Berardi, Ph.D.
Research and Authentication: Mary Brinker, Mary Adair Dockery

Table of contents

64001

CRISTÓBAL DE VILLALPANDO (Mexican, 1649-1714)
Portrait of Christ, 1690
Oil on canvas
18 x 11 inches (45.7 x 27.9 cm)
Signed and dated lower right: *Villalpando / 1690*

Estimate: $3,000-$5,000

64002

Circle of GEORGE ROMNEY (British, 1734-1802)
Portrait of a Man, Purportedly Arthur Young, Secretary of Agriculture
Oil on canvas
50 x 40 inches (127 x 101.6 cm)

PROVENANCE:
Collection Sir Horatio Davies, London;
Leggatt Brothers, London;
Arthur Tooth, London (as George Romney);
Doyle New York, *Important English and Continental,* January 22, 2003,
lot 159;
Acquired by the present owner from the above.

Estimate: $10,000-$15,000

64003

FROM THE ESTATE OF KENNETH KENDALL, LOS ANGELES, CALIFORNIA

HENRY RAEBURN (British, 1756-1823)
Portrait of General Henry Wynyard, circa 1811-1819
Oil on canvas
30 x 25-1/2 inches (76.2 x 64.8 cm)

PROVENANCE:

By inheritance to William Cornwallis West (1835-1917), Newlands Manor, Lymington, Hampshire, by 1895 (partial label verso);
With Captain Jack Spink, London, in 1923-24 (per Witt Library photo archive, Courtauld Institute, University of London);
With Ehrich Galleries, New York, acquired from above c. 1923-24;
Paul Rodman Mabury, Los Angeles, acquired from above 1930 (label verso);
Los Angeles County Museum of Art, Los Angeles, CA, bequest of Paul Rodman Mabury in 1939, acc. no. 39.12.18 (label verso);
Sotheby Parke-Bernet, Los Angeles, "An Auction of Property Deaccessioned by the Los Angeles County Museum of Art," November 7, 1977, lot 98;
Kenneth Kendall, Los Angeles, CA, acquired from the above.

LITERATURE:

W. Armstrong, *Sir Henry Raeburn*, 1901, p. 114;
J. Greig, *Sir Henry Raeburn, R.A. his life and works, with a catalog of his pictures*, 1911, p. 63, noting the Cornwallis West provenance;
Los Angeles County Museum of Art, *Paul Rodman Mabury Catalog*, 1939, ill. p. 13.
Los Angeles County Museum of Art, *A Catalogue of Flemish, German, Dutch and English Paintings, XV-XVIII Century, II,* 1954, cat. no. 94, p. 86; plate 94 (black and white), with first name of sitter erroneously given as "Harvey" instead of "Henry": "Portrait of General Harvey Wynyard. In half-length, he faces the spectator, bare-headed but in uniform; neutral background."

EXHIBITED:

Grafton Gallery, "Scottish Old Masters," 1895, lent by West;
Los Angeles County Museum of Art, Temporary installation of the Mabury Collection, March 1939.

James Greig's 1911 inventory of Raeburn's paintings incorrectly lists the sitter of this handsome portrait as "Colonel Harvey Wynyard," which has been repeated throughout much of the painting's history. Documentation of early 19th-century British regiments records not a Harvey Wynyard, but rather a *Henry* Wynyard (1761-1839), who had a successful military career. He was made Brevet Colonel in 1796, 3rd Major in 1801, Major-General in 1802, 2nd Major in 1804, Lieutenant-General in 1808, Colonel of the 64th Foot Regiment in 1809, and General in 1819. The Los Angeles County Museum of Art's label on the painting's stretcher bears a hand-written note correcting the name of the sitter. A portrait after Sir Henry Raeburn of General Henry Wynyard measuring 74 x 61 cm. is in the collection of Sizergh Castle, Cumbria, England, a National Trust property. An early owner of the present portrait by Raeburn, Colonel William Cornwallis West (1835-1917), was a British Parliamentarian and Honorary Colonel in the 4th Battalion of the Royal Welch Fusiliers

Estimate: $8,000-$12,000

64004

JOHN SAINT-HÉLIER LANDER (British, 1869-1944)
Portrait of Major Romer in the Uniform of the Band of the Scots Guard, 1938
Oil on canvas
48 x 36-1/4 inches (121.9 x 91.9 cm)
Signed and dated lower right: *John S'Hélier Lander / 1938*

PROVENANCE:
Lyon and Turnbull, Edinburgh, *Fine Paintings*, December 7, 2001, lot 97.

Estimate: $4,000-$6,000

64005

DAVID ALISON (British, 1882-1955)
Portrait of a Gentleman, 1928
Oil on canvas
30 x 25 inches (76.2 x 63.5 cm)
Signed and dated lower right: *David Alison / 1928*

Estimate: $4,000-$6,000

64006

Studio of SIR THOMAS LAWRENCE (British, 1769-1830)
Portrait of Richard Hart Davis, M.P. (1769-1842), after 1815 - circa 1830
Oil on canvas (lined)
31-1/2 x 25 inches (80.0 x 63.5 cm)

PROVENANCE:
Ehrich-Newhouse Galleries, New York, New York (by 1935);
Private collection, Kansas (purchased from the above on November 16, 1935, extant bill of sale);
Alan Barnes Fine Art, Dallas (purchased from the above in 2006).

There are two labels on the reverse of the frame: a hand-lettered number "16" which appears to be an exhibition or collection label, and a small paste-down with red border with the handwritten numbers in ballpoint pen "4987." The latter resembles a museum transit label.

This dashing portrait is one of four or possibly five versions produced after a much-admired likeness of Bristol merchant Richard Hart Davis, M.P. painted by Sir Thomas Lawrence in 1815.

The specific half-length presentation Lawrence chose to portray Richard Hart Davis was one he used to great effect during the 1810s for men who were political celebrities and public figures. The painter placed his subject against a dark background, highlighting the face and showing only a mysterious flash of brilliance somewhere in the darkness behind him. Usually the sitter wore, at Lawrence's request, a costume featuring a passage of searing red so that the portrait would contain an accent of irresistible visual richness. Lawrence's sharp illumination of the face accentuated clearcut lines, giving the impression, as it does here, of intellectual strength and physical vigor. Lawrence's remarkable portraits of *Arthur Wellesley, 1st Duke of Wellington* (Wellington Museum, Apsley House, London) and the great Neoclassical sculptor *Antonio Canova* (Pinacoteca di Casa Canova, Museo Gipsoteca Canoviana di Possagno, Italy) possess the same painterly conventions characterizing this portrait of Richard Hart Davis.

Lawrence and Davis were both born in Bristol within three years of each other-the painter in 1766 and Davis in 1769. Over the years the two men became friends when their lives intersected through a mutual love of art. Both were avid and discerning collectors, Davis of outstanding Old Master paintings which became available as a result of the Napoleonic invasions and for which he was willing to pay a king's ransom to acquire, and Lawrence of Old Master drawings. Diarist Joseph Farington reported that by 1813 (two years before Lawrence painted his portrait) Davis has already spent £100,000 on his art collection. Following financial reversals of 1818, Richard Hart Davis sold his collection *en bloc* to Sir Philip Miles of Leigh Court just outside Bristol, which became the nucleus of the celebrated Leigh Court Collection, dispersed in 1899.

Richard Hart Davis was a self-made man, the third son of Henry Davis of Bristol and his second wife, Marianna, only daughter and heiress of Major Hart-Davis of Grantham, County Lincolnshire. He and his wife, Sarah Whittingham of Earlsmead, had four children who lived to adulthood (two daughters, Clementina and Louisa; two sons, Hart and Richard Vaughan). A Member of Parliament for the notoriously corrupt borough of Colchester in 1807-12 and for Bristol in 1812-31 (six consecutive parliaments), Richard Hart Davis was a political associate of Lord Liverpool, the Prime Minister who was instrumental in the foundation of the National Gallery, London. By age 28 he had become a partner in Harford's Bank in Bristol, and in 1803 joined the Society of Merchant Venturers. In 1810, according to Lord Dunstanville, Davis was known to have become a fabulously successful commercial speculator who had managed to gain possession of all the Spanish wool in the Kingdom, reportedly making £200,000. His coup in cornering the wool market doubtless helped his ability to buy pictures, to commission the 1815 portrait of himself and at least four other family members from Thomas Lawrence (and quite probably studio versions of these as well), and to purchase real estate. Farington remarked quite pointedly that unlike most Bristol merchants, Richard Hart Davis lived at large expense and had four residences: one in Bristol, one near Bristol (Mortimer House in Clifton), and two in London (one in Grosvenor Square). Certainly four children and four homes could easily account for the multiple versions of this commanding portrait by Lawrence which have appeared on the market during the 1920s and 30s, and again during the past two decades.

The painting which is currently held to be the primary version of the Richard Hart Davis portrait by Lawrence was sold through Sotheby's, London, The British Sale, 22 March 2000, lot 85. The last owner of that painting was the distinguished publisher, author, and descendant of the sitter, Sir Rupert Hart-Davis, who died in 1999 (he hyphenated his name). According to Kenneth Garlick's 1989 catalogue raisonné of Lawrence (cat. no. 391), the portrait measured 30 x 25 inches and descended uninterrupted in the Hart-Davis family to then-owner Sir Rupert. When the work was sold at Sotheby's in 2000, however, the cataloguing deviated in places from Garlick's documentation of it. The dimensions were given instead as 29 ½ x 24 ½ in. and the provenance states that the work descended in the family to the Rev. R. H. Hart Davis, until it was sold at Christie's, 14th July 1922, lot 24 to Partridge for £787.10. These discrepancies raise the question of whether versions of this portrait, and/or their histories were conflated. (The 1922 sale also included portraits of Richard Hart Davis's son Hart Hart Davis and his wife Charlotte. The Hart Hart Davis portrait in the 1922 sale is certainly a replica of the primary version which was made for Eton College, where it has remained ever since. It was commissioned by Richard Hart Davis in 1809 from Thomas Lawrence as his son's Eton "Leaving Portrait.")

According to Garlick's 1989 catalogue (see mention in note to cat. no. 391), there is a copy of Lawrence's *Portrait of Richard Hart Davis* in the Mansion House, Bristol (now residence of Bristol's Lord Mayor). A third version of the *Portrait of Richard Hart Davis* is reproduced in the Witt photographic archive of The Courtauld Institute of Art, London (fiche 2124, box 1418) as having been in the collection of a Reverend W. H. Powell of Bristol in 1937. Powell loaned it to an exhibition of Lawrence's paintings in Bristol in 1937. This portrait, measuring a slightly narrower 30 x 23 ½ inches, appears from photographs to be quite similar to the present work. Whether the Powell version and the Mansion House version could be one and the same painting is unknown at this writing. A fourth version of the portrait measuring 30 x 25 inches is reproduced in the Witt photo archives (fiche 2124, box 1418) as having been on the art market with G. Arnot, London in 1929. The sharpness of the photo makes a clear reading of the handling difficult, though it seems somewhat softer and closer perhaps to the version which sold at Sotheby's in 2000. A possible fifth version measuring 30.1 x 25.2 inches-and the only one to date which was sold as "Attributed to Thomas Lawrence" rather than with a full attribution-fetched $8,087 at Neumeister on September 19, 1990, lot 578. The work was not illustrated. Additionally, an oil study for the *Portrait of Richard Hart Davis* was part of lot 13 in the Thomas Lawrence studio sale, 18th June 1831 (possibly sold at Tajan, Paris, 18 December 1995, lot 43).

During the same year he painted Richard Hart Davis, Thomas Lawrence embarked upon a royal commission from the Prince Regent that not only made his career, but reaped for him tremendous and unprecedented financial rewards: a series of portraits of the allied leaders following their triumph over Napoleon for the so-called Waterloo Chamber at Windsor Castle. To accomplish this remarkable body of work, Lawrence was required to travel abroad extensively—to Aachen, Vienna, and Rome. When he returned to England in 1820, he was knighted and elected president of the Royal Academy. The confidence with which he painted the *Portrait of Richard Hart Davis* characterizes his achievements going forward. Moreover, it contains that idiosyncratic blend of sensuous design and romantic longing with the requisite formality of an official image that was to become Lawrence's most personal contribution to the history of portraiture.

Estimate: $15,000-$20,000

64007

PROPERTY FROM A DALLAS PRIVATE COLLECTION

EDWARD LADELL (British, 1821-1886)
Still Life with Ceramic Jug, Wine Glass, and Tazza with Fruit
Oil on canvas
20 x 16 inches (50.8 x 40.6 cm)
Initialed lower right: *EL*

PROVENANCE:
Christie's, New York, *19th-Century European Paintings, Drawings, Watercolors & Sculpture*, November 2, 1995, lot 206 (label verso).

Estimate: $8,000-$12,000

64008

PROPERTY FROM A PRIVATE TEXAS COLLECTION

After JEAN LOUIS GREGOIRE (French, 1840-1890)
Young Woman with Lyre
Bronze with brown patina
15-1/2 x 16-1/2 inches (39.4 x 41.9 cm)
Signed on base: *L. Gregoire*

Estimate: $2,000-$3,000

64009

PROPERTY FROM A PRIVATE TEXAS COLLECTION

Attributed to JONATHAN RICHARDSON (British, 1665-1745)
Man in Green Cap
Oil on canvas
19 x 15-1/4 inches (48.3 x 38.7 cm)

PROVENANCE:
Arthur Ackermann & Son, Inc., New York;
Private collection, Washington, D.C., purchased from the above, May 24, 1965;
Thence by descent to the present owner.

Estimate: $6,000-$9,000

64010

PROPERTY FROM A PRIVATE COLLECTION, BALTIMORE, MARYLAND

LOUISE RAYNER (British, 1829-1924)
Temple Bar
Watercolor and gouache on paper
13-3/4 x 10-1/4 inches (34.9 x 26.0 cm)
Signed lower right: *Louise Rayner*

PROVENANCE:
Purnell Art Company, Baltimore, Maryland;
Mr. and Mrs. C.O. Briddell, Baltimore Maryland, purchased from the above,
July 18, 1958;
By descent to the present owners.

Estimate: $5,000-$7,000

64011

PROPERTY FROM A PRIVATE COLLECTION, BALTIMORE, MARYLAND

LOUISE RAYNER (British, 1829-1924)
High Street, Salisbury
Watercolor and gouache on paper
8-1/2 x 6-1/4 inches (21.6 x 15.9 cm)
Signed lower right: *Louise Rayner*

PROVENANCE:
Richard Green Fine Paintings, Ltd., London;
Mr. and Mrs. C.O. Briddell, Baltimore, Maryland, purchased from the above,
December 20, 1966;
By descent to the present owners.

Estimate: $3,000-$5,000

64012

PROPERTY FROM A PROMINENT COLLECTION, BALTIMORE, MARYLAND

LOUISE RAYNER (British, 1829-1924)
Christ Church, Oxford
Watercolor and gouache on paper
20-3/4 x 29-3/4 inches (52.7 x 75.6 cm)
Signed lower right: *Louise Rayner*

PROVENANCE:
Purnell Art Company, Baltimore, Maryland;
Mr. and Mrs. C.O. Briddell, Baltimore, Maryland, purchased from the above, November 10, 1961;
By descent to the present owners.

Estimate: $15,000-$25,000

64013

ROBERT SALMON (Scottish/American, 1775-1844)
The Estridge in Two Views Off Dover, 1800
Oil on canvas
26-1/2 x 43 inches (67.3 x 109.2 cm)
Signed and dated lower left: *R. SALMON / 1800*

PROVENANCE:
Private collection, 1920-1970;
Schillay and Rehs Gallery, New York City, New York;
Private collection, purchased from the above, 1970;
Vallejo Gallery, Newport Beach, California, 2010;
Private collection, acquired from the above.

The longtime owner of this important work by Robert Salmon from 1970 to 2010 was a well-known marine art collector and great friend of Glen S. Foster, who assembled one of the most important American collections of marine art during the last half of the 20th century. The two men were yachting buddies and frequently competed against one another for prize examples of marine art.

This serene and luminous scene of the ship Estridge shown off the coast Dover is one of two earliest-known works by Salmon. Both this work, which shows the ship Estridge in two views, and *Two Armed Merchantmen Leaving Whitehaven Harbor* were executed in 1800.

The Estridge is recorded in a Dundee archive as having been built in 1777 by Master George Deuchars. It weighed 312 tons, and was owned by John Hume when it was put into service as a whaler in 1822. This information matches the vessel physically, but in Salmon's painting, the ship is definitely under a naval command. There was also an earlier vessel in the Royal British Navy of the same name, late in the 18th Century, but it was a smaller "fire ship."

The hull construction of the Estridge is in the style of the flush-deck frigates that would come to dominate in the War of 1812, but without as much armament. The ship is flying a Red Squadron pennant on the main, and in company with a large brig of the same allegiance, indicating naval duty in the Napoleonic Era. It seems that in Salmon's painting, the Estridge is a merchant vessel under naval contract, since it doesn't appear in the official roll that was very precise.

In 1795 the Estridge was involved in a collision with the British warship "Active."

Estimate: $125,000-$175,000

64014

EDGAR HUNT (British, 1876-1953)
Barnyard Scene, 1931
Oil on canvas
11 x 16 inches (27.9 x 40.6 cm)
Signed and dated lower right: *E Hunt 1931*

PROVENANCE:
Private collection, San Francisco, acquired circa 1970s;
Thence by descent to the present owner.

Estimate: $8,000-$12,000

64015

HENRY HETHERINGTON EMMERSON (British, 1831-1895)
The Farmer's Daughter, 1872
Oil on canvas
39-3/8 x 64-1/8 inches (100.1 x 162.9 cm)
Signed and dated lower center: *H. H. Emmerson 1872*

PROVENANCE:
Barkreach Tweedy (label verso);
Thomas Agnew and Sons, Liverpool (label verso);
Henry H. Beaven, purchased on March 24, 1914 per label verso;
Private collection, California.

EXHIBITED:
The Royal Academy, London, 1873 (per label verso).

Estimate: $10,000-$15,000

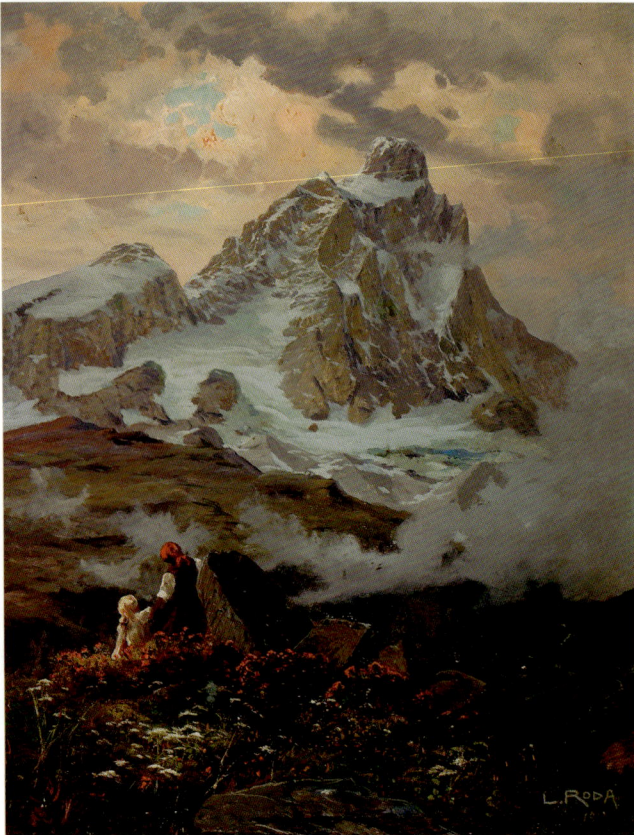

64016

LEONARDO RODA (Italian, 1868-1933)
The Matterhorn, 1918
Oil on canvas
40-1/2 x 32 inches (102.9 x 81.3 cm)
Signed and dated lower right: *L. Roda / 1918*

PROVENANCE:
Private collection, Corpus Christi, Texas.

Estimate: $6,000-$9,000

64017

EUGENIO ZAMPIGHI (Italian, 1859-1944)
Follies of Old Age
Watercolor on board
21-1/2 x 14-1/2 inches (54.6 x 36.8 cm)
Signed lower left: *E Zampighi*

Estimate: $3,000-$5,000

64018

PROPERTY FROM A PRIVATE TEXAS COLLECTION

FRANCESCO PELUSO (Italian, 1836-1936)
The Courtship
Oil on canvas
26 x 19-1/2 inches (66.0 x 49.5 cm)
Signed lower right: *F. Peluso*

PROVENANCE:
C.J. Wrightsman, Fort Worth, Texas, purchased circa 1920s;
Mrs. Mildred Warren Carey, Fort Worth, Texas, acquired from the above, circa 1959;
Thence by descent to the present owner.

Estimate: $5,000-$7,000

64019

PIO RICCI (Italian, 1850-1919)
The Temptress
Oil on canvas
28-1/2 x 16-1/2 inches (72.4 x 41.9 cm)
Signed lower left: *Pio Ricci*

Estimate: $10,000-$15,000

64020

Attributed to JOACHIM FERDINAND RICHARDT (Danish, 1819-1895)
Village Scene with Church
Oil on canvas
30 x 50 inches (76.2 x 127 cm)

The church depicted in this large landscape is consistent with the architecture of John McComb, Jr, (American, 1763-1853), who enjoyed a successful career designing buildings in New York City and along the east coast.

Estimate: $7,000-$10,000

64021

CARL FREDERICK SORENSEN (Danish, 1818-1879)
Amsterdam Skating Scene, 1848
Oil on panel
12-1/2 x 16 inches (31.8 x 40.6 cm)
Signed and dated lower left: *Sorensen '48*

Estimate: $4,000-$6,000

64022

PEDER MORK MÖNSTED (Danish, 1859-1941)
Road to New Battle, 1879
Oil on canvas
16-3/4 x 22-3/4 inches (42.5 x 57.8 cm)
Signed and dated lower center: *P. Mönsted 79*

PROVENANCE:
Private collection, Denmark;
Acquired by the present owner from the above, circa 1985.

Estimate: $7,000-$9,000

64023

VALENTIN DE ZUBIAURRE (Spanish, 1879-1963)
Aqueduct of Segovia, circa 1920
Oil on canvas
32 x 38 inches (81.3 x 96.5 cm)
Signed lower left: *: VALENTIN DE ZUBIAURRE :*

PROVENANCE:
Dudensing Galleries, New York;
Purchased from the above by the Dallas Art Association through the Munger Fund, 1926;
The Dallas Museum of Art, Dallas, Texas (1926.2.M), until circa 1985 when deaccessioned;
Christie's, New York October 30, 1985, lot 204 (partial label verso);
Private collection, New York.

EXHIBITED (all loans from the Dudensing Galleries):
Cincinnati Art Museum, Eden Park, Cincinnati, Ohio, "Spanish Paintings by Valentin and Ramon de Zubiaurre," October 1026, no. 30;
Brooks Memorial Art Gallery, Overton Park, Memphis, Tennessee, "Exhibition of Spanish Paintings," September 12-27, 1926, no. 30;
Melrose Court, Dallas, Texas, "Paintings by the Brothers De Zubiaurre (Ramon & Valentin)," November 8-14, 1926, organized by the Dallas Art Association.

Spanish painters Valentin and Ramon de Zubiaurre were the sons of Valentin de Zubiaurre, a Professor of Madrid's Music Conservatory and Director of the Royal Chapel there. Though they were born deaf and dumb, the two brothers soon started to draw and paint with extraordinary facility after a short training at the School of Fine Arts in Madrid. They then went to Paris where they were profoundly influenced by the paintings of their French contemporaries, whose Modernist tendencies are reflected in their simplification of form and composition into strong, basic geometries.

Upon moving back to their Basque homeland in Northern Spain (Gavay/Vizcaya), Valentin and Ramon became famous for their depictions of Basque folklore, indigenous handicrafts that are featured in the foreground still lifes of their portraits, and societal characters. Their interest in regional Spanish subjects has affinity with the well-known paintings of their countryman, Sorolla. But unlike Sorolla who was interested, as John Singer Sargent and Giovanni Boldini were, in describing his subjects with flashy bravura brushwork and its sparkling effects, the de Zubiaurre brothers emphasized the sculptural solidity of their forms with smooth application of paint. The difference in approach creates moods that are worlds apart. Many writers have associated the work of Valentin and Ramon with that of the Flemish primitives, not only because of their focus on peasant subjects, but because of their insistent realism and the additive nature of their compositions. Others see an association between the powerful stillness and austerity in their work and the brothers' deafness.

Valentin's *Aqueduct of Segovia* was shown on a nationwide tour of the de Zubiaurre brothers' work mounted in the mid-1920s by the Dudensing Galleries of New York. In those days, works shown by art dealers in museum settings were for sale, as these were. When this painting was exhibited in 1926 by Dudensing Galleries in Dallas at the Melrose Court (now the Warwick Melrose Hotel on Oak Lawn), it was purchased by the Dallas Art Association. A work very similar in subject to this painting by Ramon de Zubiaurre, entitled *Typos de Segovia*, but with a different still life and the male and female flanking figures reversed, sold at auction at Sotheby's, London, June 21, 1989, lot 636 (oil on canvas, 99 x 99 inches). A comparison of the two similar compositions illustrates that Valentin's work has a greater sophistication in its draftsmanship and finish.

A writer for *Art Digest* wrote appreciatively of Valentin's depictions of Castilian subjects [including Segovia] in January 1921, p. 173: "The most remarkable thing in [his] work...is the value acquired by the color of his buildings. Castile, with its astounding twilights, has filled Valentin de Zubiaurre with the intoxication of its flaming skies, stretching wide over the parched lands below them. The clouds, so red, so inconceivably red...and the soil implacably yellow or light brown and the sharp greens of the women's skirts, and the cloaks of the men, with their big round hats, so obstinately sombre--all these, with the abrupt standing-out of the silhouettes against the bare, wild landscape, have served to form, little by little, surely, and for always, the palette of an artist the meditation of whose vision of things amounts to an act of faith. And even in works [that] are not due to direct contact with Castile itself, there is an exaltation which reflects the colour of Castile, with its blood-red night-falls. Certain of Nature's magnificences have never been better expressed..."

Many thanks to Leigh Arnold, Research Project Coordinator, Department of Contemporary Art, Dallas Museum of Art, for her kind assistance in researching the provenance and exhibition history for this lot at the DMA. We are also grateful to Christine Edmondson, librarian at the Ingalls Library, Cleveland Museum of Art, Cleveland, Ohio for her generous assistance in securing research materials relevant to the American tour of the de Zubiaurre brothers' work staged by the Dudensing Galleries during the 1920s.

Estimate: $15,000-$25,000

64024

JULIUS ROSE (German, 1828-1911)
Alpine Landscape with River
Oil on canvas
18-1/2 x 27 inches (47.0 x 68.6 cm)
Signed lower left: *Rose*

Estimate: $5,000-$7,000

64025

ANTON HLAVACEK (Austrian, 1842-1926)
Canoeing on a Mountain Lake, circa 1920
Oil on canvas
39 x 62 inches (99.1 x 157.5 cm)
Signed lower right: *Hlavacek*

Estimate: $7,000-$10,000

64026

ALEXEJ ALEXEJEWITSCH CHARLAMOFF (Russian, 1842-1930)
Guinevere and Lancelot
Oil on canvas
28-3/4 x 21-1/2 inches (73.0 x 54.6 cm)
Signed lower right: *A. Harlamoff*

Estimate: $12,000-$16,000

64027

FERDINAND LEEKE (German, 1859-1959)
Lohengrin: Act III
Oil on canvas
39-3/4 x 47-1/2 inches (101.0 x 120.7 cm)
Signed lower left: *Ferd Leeke...*

In the tradition of the great nineteenth-century German academic painters, Ferdinand Leeke, who trained with Johann Herterich at the Munich Academy, specialized in large-scale historical, allegorical, and mythological paintings. His facility in rendering highly dramatic narratives caught the attention of Siegfried Wagner, son of the famous composer Richard Wagner, and around 1889 Siegfried commissioned Leeke to paint ten episodes from Wagner's principal operas: *Rienzi*, Act IV, Scene II; *Der fliegende Holländer*, Act III, Final Scene; *Tannhäuser*, Act III, Scene I; *Lohengrin*, Act III, Final Scene; *Das Rheingold*, Scene II; *Die Walküre*, Act I; *Siegfried*, Act II; *Götterdämmerung*, Act III; *Tristan und Isolde*, Act II; and *Die Meistersinger von Nürnberg*, Act III. Leeke completed the commission by 1898, and the following year, the Bavarian printer Franz Hanfstaengel, using the novel six-color photogravure process, reproduced the paintings as posters. Indeed, the popularity of this series compelled Leeke to explore variations on Wagnerian subjects for the remainder of his career.

Heritage is pleased to offer this lot, one of Leeke's interpretations of Wagner's 1848 opera *Lohengrin*, based on the medieval German legend about a knight of the Holy Grail who can only save maiden Elsa from a false accusation of murder as long as she never inquires about his true identity. Where the *Lohengrin* painting commissioned by Siegfried Wagner depicted the final scene of the opera, Elsa's demise from a broken heart in the presence of her attendants and accusers, the Heritage version captures the equally famous Act III, Scene I, or "The Bridal Chamber." Spotlighting the couple within the cocoon of their bedroom, Leeke shows Elsa's regret after having asked her beloved husband the fatal question about his name. More intimate than Leeke's multi-figure landscapes, *Lohengrin* maintains dramatic power in its reduction of the critical moment to the lovers' facial expressions and gestures.

Estimate: $4,000-$6,000

64028

School of CLAUDE LORRAIN (French, 1604-1682)
Shepherds at the Shrine of Artemis
Oil on canvas
36 x 29-3/4 inches (91.4 x 75.6 cm)

Estimate: $5,000-$7,000

64029

BLAISE ALEXANDRE DESGOFFE (French, 1830-1901)
Still Life with Potted Flower
Oil on canvas
12-3/4 x 9-3/4 inches (32.4 x 24.8 cm)
Signed into the composition upper left: *Blaise Desgoffe*

Estimate: $2,500-$3,500

64030

PROPERTY FROM A PRIVATE COLLECTION, OREGON

BRITON RIVIERE (British, 1840-1920)
A Stern Chase is a Long Chase, 1876
Oil on canvas
37 x 72 inches (94.0 x 182.9 cm)
Signed and dated lower right: *B Riviere / 1876*

PROVENANCE:
Private collection, Oregon, acquired circa 1880;
Kenneth MacKenzie Clark Neill, Oregon, by descent;
By descent through the family to the present owner.

Estimate: $5,000-$7,000

64031

PIERRE ARTHUR GAILLARD (French, 19th Century)
Un Coin de Pré en Fleurs (A Corner of the Field in Bloom), 1892
Oil on canvas
61-3/4 x 99 inches (156.8 x 251.5 cm)
Signed and dated lower left: *P. A. Gaillard 1892*

PROVENANCE:
Private collection, California.

EXHIBITED:
possibly Paris Salon,1892, no. 724 as "Un coin de Pré en Fleurs"

Estimate: $20,000-$30,000

64032

PROPERTY FROM THE LUCIEN ABRAMS COLLECTION

PIERRE-AUGUSTE RENOIR (French, 1841-1919)
Le Bouquet, 1910
Oil on canvas
17 x 12-1/2 inches (43.2 x 31.8 cm)
Signed lower left: *Renoir*
Two paste-down labels on stretcher bars bearing stock numbers: no. 4362 and no. 10401

PROVENANCE:
Durand-Ruel, Inc., New York;
Lucien Abrams, Old Lyme, CT, purchased from the above on September 20, 1933, with stock number 4367 indicated on preserved copy of photostatic invoice;
By continuous descent in the family to the current owner.

LITERATURE:
Gallery Gardens, Dallas Museum of Fine Arts, Dallas, Texas, 1963, ill in black and white, cat. no. 43 (erroneously listed as "Collection of the Marion Koogler McNay Art Institute, The Lucien Abrams Collection").

EXHIBITED:
The Marion Koogler McNay Art Museum (known as The McNay Art Museum, since 1963), San Antonio, Texas, on extended loan from 1961 until December 2000 (label verso);*
"Gallery Gardens," Dallas Museum of Fine Arts, Dallas, Texas, in cooperation with the Dallas Garden Club of the Dallas Woman's Club, February 23 - March 24, 1963, no. 43;
The Old Jail Museum, Albany, Texas, on extended loan from December 2000 until November 2010.

Estimate: $500,000-$700,000

Pierre-Auguste Renoir painted this exuberant bouquet of pink and yellow roses in 1910, just three years after he and his family relocated permanently to Cagnes-sur-Mer on the Mediterranean. The move from rainy Paris to warm and sunny Cagnes in 1907 opened the late great chapter of Renoir's career as one of the foremost French Impressionists. For the remaining 12 years of his life, the painter saw the market for his work in all genres-landscapes, still lifes, portraits, and figure compositions, most notably his female nudes and bathers-begin its ascent to the top rung of desirability of any French Impressionist. By the 1930s, when this bouquet was acquired by the grandfather of the present owner, Renoir's market was exploding in the United States, as his savvy dealer and champion, Durand-Ruel, was selling to important collectors, American millionaires, and major American museums for record sums.

The kinder climate and beautiful surroundings in Cagnes, where Renoir painted Le Bouquet, alleviated the discomfort of the painter's chronic health problems (nerve damage in his right eye, respiratory illnesses, and the severe rheumatoid arthritis crippling his hands), and inspired him artistically. Then in his sixties, and flourishing financially at last, thanks in part to his resourceful dealer Paul Durand-Ruel, Renoir was able to afford a nine-acre estate known as "Les Collettes."[1] With its picturesque views of the Cote d'Azur and its old stone farmhouse surrounded by olive groves, vineyards, orchards, and flowering gardens, Les Collettes was a true painter's paradise. Over the next decade, Renoir and his wife Aline reshaped many of the gardens, for example, adding roses, bougainvillea, and dahlias to existing fields of daisies and lavender, and further beautified the landscape that inspired his last great canvases. Too, Renoir was re-experiencing the joys of fatherhood; Aline gave birth to their third son, Coco, in 1901, and raised him in this idyllic environment.

Renoir's Roses

At Les Collettes Renoir devoted special attention to roses, which had always been his favorite flower.[2] As a young apprentice, he had painted roses on Sevres and Limoges porcelain, later on decorative fans, and roses feature prominently in his still lifes and figurative works from the 1880s and '90s -- as corsages, hair ornaments, and bouquets. At Les Collettes, Renoir and Aline designed a formal garden of alternating orange trees and rose bushes, both old-fashioned varieties and the newer Hybrid Teas, and Aline kept fresh-cut roses throughout the house as a ready source for her husband's still-life compositions. Whether neatly arranged in gardens, snaking up the farmhouse, or spilling over retaining walls, roses became so linked with Les Collettes that a local rose grower, Henri Estable, in 1909 named a new breed "Painter Renoir" in honor of his friend.[3]

In *Le Bouquet*, and similar still lifes from the period, Renoir's fully opened clump of "Painter Renoirs" in a bulbous blue iridescent vase shares the same voluptuousness of form and quivering brushwork as his monumental bathers and mythological nudes from this same period. As the late art connoisseur and museum director Ted Pillsbury further described *The Bouquet*, "The short brushstrokes vibrate with energy, and the colors create a rich pattern of horticultural exuberance."[4] Indeed, Renoir's way of painting flowers and nudes was very similar because flowers and flesh were conceptually linked in his mind. Renoir told art dealer Ambroise Vollard that his fascination with flowers, particularly roses, lay in their specific association with the body:

"[Flower paintings] are experiments with flesh tints that I make for my nudes.[5] Renoir also confessed: "I find mental relaxation in painting flowers. I am not as tense as I am in front of the model. When I paint flowers, I try different tones and daring values. I would not venture to do it with a figure, for fear of spoiling everything." In the exquisite palette he used to render the roses in *Le Bouquet*, Renoir explored a wide range of skin tones, from creamy whites to soft pinks to near reds, but also infused the blossoms with daring chromatic notes of steel blue, grassy green and shots of electric orange and chocolate brown.

Renoir Collector Lucien Abrams

Renoir's skills as a colorist can be fully appreciated in *Le Bouquet* because the 101 year-old painting is in a superb state of preservation. It has been in the continuous ownership of a single family from the time it was purchased on September 20, 1933 from the New York branch of Durand-Ruel Galleries by Lucien Abrams of Old Lyme, Connecticut, to the present day. Abrams (1870-1941) was an American collector and painter in his own right. At the same time that Renoir was painting *Le Bouquet* at Les Collettes, in fact, the Kansas-born, Dallas-raised Abrams was himself studying Impressionist technique in France. Art historian Michael Grauer has noted of Abrams' career: "Following his graduation from Princeton University in 1892, Abrams was intent on becoming a painter. He first studied at the Art Students League in New York and then at the Academie Julian in Paris, with a short stint at J.M.W. Whistler's school in Paris. Abrams returned to the United States in 1900 living in Fort Worth, Texas, for six months, and painted in New York and Rockport, Massachusetts. During his extensive travels throughout Europe until about 1914, he painted in Belgium, Provence, Brittany, Southern France, Italy, Spain, and Algeria. In museums he studied the Old Masters and developed a keen sense of connoisseurship."

"From 1902 to 1914," Grauer continues, "Abrams exhibited annually in Paris at the Salon d'Automne and the Salon des Indépendants. In 1914, he and his wife, Charlotte Gina Onillon, a Parisienne, built a home in Old Lyme, and divided their time between there, his family's home in Dallas, and a winter home in San Antonio. Abrams also exhibited at the Art Institute of Chicago annual in 1899; the Pennsylvania Academy of the Fine Arts annual in 1903 and 1911; the National Academy of Design annual in 1908; the Lyme Art Association from 1915 until the 1930s; and in numerous Texas venues. Abrams had one-man exhibitions at Pabst Galleries in San Antonio (1930) and at Durand-Ruel Galleries, New York (1934).[6]

As an artist himself, Abrams had enormous appreciation for the achievement of Renoir, but allowed himself to be guided by Durand-Ruel, from whom he acquired a notable collection of Impressionist paintings, most by Renoir, which the gallery had acquired directly from the artist. Letters from Durand-Ruel encouraged Abrams to come view the latest shipments of Renoirs from Paris. Between 1929 and 1938, Abrams purchased a total of fourteen Renoir paintings from Durand-Ruel, many of these dating to Renoir's years in Cagnes, including: the present *Bouquet*, 1910; *Baigneuse assise*, 1905; *Bust de femme, brune*, 1910; *Citron et tasse, Cagnes*, 1912 (sale and partial gift to the McNay Art Museum, San Antonio, in 2010, brokered by Ted Pillsbury of Heritage Auctions); *The Farm at Les Collettes, Cagnes*, 1914 (bequeathed by Charlotte Gina Abrams to the Metropolitan Museum in 1961 in memory of her husband, Lucien); *Femme nue, couchee*, 1914; *Buste de jeune fille*, 1917; and *Femme au chapeau de paille*, 1917.[7] Given his own painting aesthetic, it is not surprising that Abrams passionately sought Renoirs, even with an impressive Matisse and a Picabia in his collection. Like Renoir, Abrams favored a vibrant palette, short brushstrokes, and dappled light effects, and he adored the flower-filled landscape as a subject, exemplified by his 1913 *Poppies and Nasturtiums, Normandie*. Abrams' granddaughter recalls having been told by her grandmother that her grandfather loved painting gardens, his own as well as those of his artist friends, as well as public parks in Dallas and untamed landscapes.[8] Surviving photographs of the interior of the Old Lyme house show Lucien Abrams' landscapes hanging alongside his Renoirs and works by his artist friends. Abrams created his own colorful Impressionist gallery, a veritable indoor Les Collettes.[9]

Indeed, Lucien Abrams' fondness for Renoir matched that of other discerning American collectors of his work during the 1930s, notably Dr. Albert C. Barnes of Marion, Pennsylvania. Perhaps more than any other Renoir enthusiast of the time, Barnes was, in particular, a champion of Renoir's late manner to which *Le Bouquet* belongs. Owing in part to the arthritis which crippled his hands but could not cripple his desire to paint, Renoir, out of physical necessity, was required to adopt a new way of working. He could no longer paint with a tight exacting network of strokes, because his hands would not cooperate, so he began working more broadly, actually stabbing at the canvas with his whole arm. What this approach created in later works like *Le Bouquet*, and in the monumental canvases Dr. Barnes acquired for his museum–the Barnes Collection–is a fascinating new sense of movement. As Albert André described Renoir's late approach: "Renoir attacks the canvas...some general outlines...then, immediately, with pure colors diluted with turpentine... he strokes the canvas rapidly and soon you see something vague appear with iridescent colors...At the second sitting...he brightens the parts that are to be luminous...Little by little he defines the forms...still permitting them to melt into each other, and one sees emerge round shapes, sparkling with the brilliance of jewels and wrapped in transparent golden shades."

In writing about a very late Renoir bouquet he himself had acquired, *Chrysanthemums in a Vase*, which is possibly Renoir's last painting, Barnes described the qualities he believed made Renoir's late work the ultimate expression of the painter's artistic genius: "The colors, by their relations to each other as well as by their individual sensuous quality, convey, independently, of the fullness of feeling in the flowers themselves, the abstract qualities of glow, iridescence, lusciousness, and voluptuous charm. A flow of glowing color seems to well up from the vase, to spread out in all directions and permeate all parts of the design, like a thick foaming liquid condensing into volumes of color as it rises."[10] While Barnes' language is ponderous, and quite the opposite Renoir's freedom of approach, it is nonetheless a remarkable tract celebrating Renoir's uncomplicated virtuosity as well as the sheer sensual pleasure he took in everything he painted.

Le Bouquet was one of nine paintings stolen in 1977 from the McNay Art Museum, which were discovered less than five miles from the museum and recovered unharmed by the police within a month of the theft. The theft was reported to the Art Loss Register.
1. B. White, *Renoir: His Life, Art, and Letters*, New York, 1984, p. 217. By 1900 his paintings were selling for upwards of 22,000 francs, topping the highest prices for a Cezanne or a Monet.
2. D. Fell, *Renoir's Garden*. New York, 1991, p. 55.
3. Ibid., p. 53-55.
4. E. Pillsbury, unpublished letter to the current owner, March 17, 2010.
5. F. Daulte, *Renoir*, Garden City, New York, 1973, p. 58.
6. M. Grauer, unpublished document for Heritage Auctions. Michael R. Grauer serves as Associate Director for Curatorial Affairs/ Curator of Art, Panhandle-Plains Historical Museum, Canyon, Texas.
7. Elfers appraisal of the Lucien Abrams Renoir collection, 1960, Abrams family archives.
8. M. Berardi, interview with the current owner, October 4, 2011.
9. M. Dockery, interview with the current owner, September 26, 2011.
10. Dr. A.C. Barnes and V. de Mazia, *The Art of Renoir*, Marion, PA, 1935, p. 437

64033

EMIL BARBARINI (Austrian, 1855-1930)
Flower Market near Vienna's St. Charles's Church
Oil on board
9-3/4 x 15 inches (24.8 x 38.1 cm)
Signed lower right: *E. Barbarini*

PROVENANCE:
Hugo Arnot Gemälde-Salon, Vienna;
M.F. Bramley, Cleveland, Ohio, purchased from the above, March 12, 1924;
Thence by descent to the present owner.

A copy of the original sales receipt from Hugo Arnot accompanies this lot.

Estimate: $3,000-$5,000

64034

PROPERTY FROM A PRIVATE COLLECTION, SAN DIEGO

DIETZ EDZARD (German, 1893-1963)
Veronica
Oil on canvas
22 x 17 inches (55.9 x 43.2 cm)
Signed lower left: *D Edzard*

PROVENANCE:
Collection of Campbell H. Elkins, Lubbock, Texas;
Jerome H. Sharpe, San Diego, California, by bequest from the above.

Estimate: $4,000-$6,000

64035

MARCEL DYF (French, 1899-1985)
Femme au Bouquet
Oil on canvas
24 x 29 inches (61.0 x 73.7 cm)
Signed lower right: *Dyf*

PROVENANCE:
Frost & Reed, London (label verso);
Burlington Paintings, London (label verso).

Estimate: $18,000-$24,000

64036

PROPERTY FROM A HOUSTON ESTATE

EDOUARD-LÉON CORTÈS (French, 1882-1969)
Madeleine, Front View
Oil on canvas
13 x 18 inches (33.0 x 45.7 cm)
Signed lower right: *EDOUARD CORTÈS*
Inscribed with Arnot Galleries inventory number on verso: *18747*

PROVENANCE:
The artist;
Arnot Galleries, New York, September 1955;
Allan Gallery, Houston, Texas, October 1955;
Stowers Furniture, San Antonio, Texas;
Private collection, Houston, Texas, purchased from the above.

Estimate: $20,000-$30,000

64037

PROPERTY FROM A HOUSTON ESTATE

EDOUARD-LÉON CORTÈS (French, 1882-1969)
The Opera
Oil on canvas
13 x 18 inches (33.0 x 45.7 cm)
Signed lower left: *EDOUARD CORTÈS*
Inscribed with Arnot Galleries inventory number on verso: *20995*

PROVENANCE:
The artist;
Arnot Galleries, New York, September 1955;
Allan Gallery, Houston, Texas, October 1955;
Stowers Furniture, San Antonio, Texas;
Private collection, Houston, Texas, purchased from the above.

Estimate: $20,000-$30,000

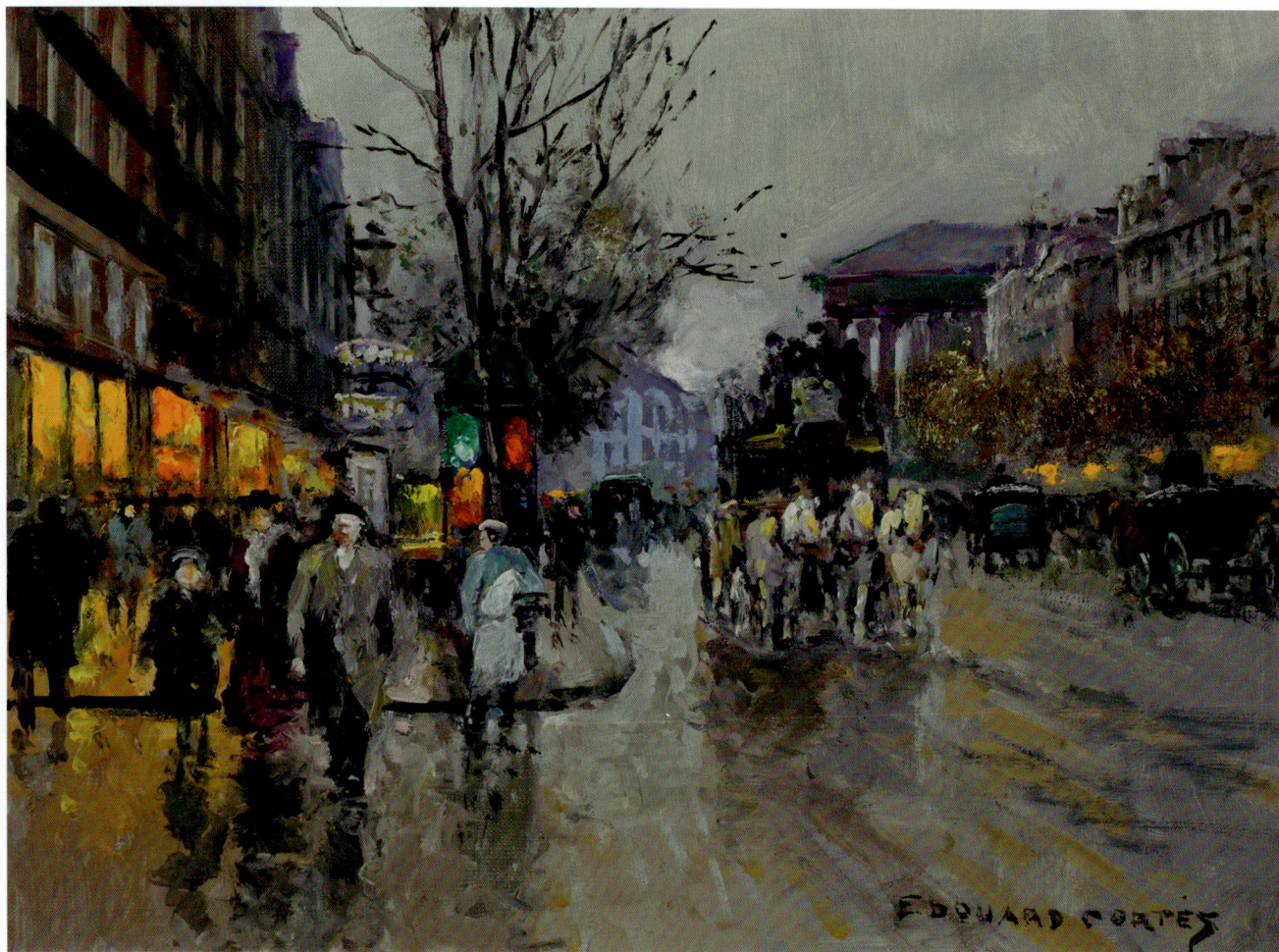

64038

EDOUARD-LÉON CORTÈS (French, 1882-1969)
Boulevard des Capucines, Paris
Oil on canvas
13 x 18 inches (33.0 x 45.7 cm)
Signed lower right: *EDOUARD CORTÈS*
Titled verso: *BOULEVARD / DE CAPUCINES / PARIS*

Estimate: $20,000-$30,000

64039

EDOUARD-LÉON CORTÈS (French, 1882-1969)

Cafe de la Paix
Oil on canvas
13 x 18 inches (33.0 x 45.7 cm)
Signed lower right: *EDOUARD CORTÈS*

PROVENANCE:
Robert Rice, Houston, Texas;
Private collection, San Diego, California, purchased from the above, 1982.

Estimate: $25,000-$35,000

64040

EDOUARD-LÉON CORTÈS (French, 1882-1969)
Parisienne Street Scene
Oil on linen
13 x 17-1/2 inches (33.0 x 44.5 cm)
Signed lower left: *EDOUARD CORTÈS*

This lot is accompanied by a certificate of authenticity from David Klein.

Estimate: $20,000-$30,000

64041

ANTOINE BLANCHARD (French, 1910-1988)
A View of the Arc de Triomphe
Oil on canvas
13 x 18 inches (33.0 x 45.7 cm)
Signed lower right: *Antoine Blanchard*

PROVENANCE:
Callan Fine Art, New Orleans.

Estimate: $5,000-$7,000

64042

JOHN E. COSTIGAN (American, 1888-1972)
Flowers in Vase
Oil on canvas
28-1/4 x 22 inches
Signed lower left: *J.E. Costigan*

Estimate: $2,000-$4,000

64043

FRENCH/BELGIAN SCHOOL (20th Century)
Three Women on a Road from the Mill, 1957
Oil on canvas
28 x 35-1/2 inches (71.1 x 90.2 cm)
Signed illegibly and dated lower right: *57*

Estimate: $2,000-$4,000

64044

YAACOV AGAM (Israeli, b. 1928)
Untitled
Color agamograph
13 x 13 inches (33.0 x 33.0 cm)
Ed. 13/99
Signed lower right: *Agam*

Estimate: $1,000-$1,500

64045

DAVID BURLIUK (Ukrainian/American, 1882-1967)
Still Life with Lilacs in a Landscape
Oil on masonite
28 x 14 inches (71.1 x 35.6 cm)
Signed lower right: *Burliuk*

PROVENANCE:
James Cox Gallery, Woodstock, New York;
Acquired by the present owner from the above.

Estimate: $10,000-$15,000

64046

ANDREI KIORESKU (Russian, b. 1964)
Winter Evening in the Village, 1997
Oil on canvas
22-1/2 x 35 inches (57.2 x 88.9 cm)
Signed lower right in Cyrillic and dated: *97*
Inscribed verso with artist's name, title, date, medium and dimensions

Estimate: $4,000-$6,000

64047

GIDEON BORJE (Swedish, 1891-1991)
Hillside Landscape with Figures
Oil on canvas
23 x 34 inches (58.4 x 86.4 cm)
Signed lower right: *G. Börje*

Estimate: $3,000-$5,000

64048

SEI KOYANAGUI (Japanese, 1896-1948)
Dogs and Bird
Oil on canvas
32 x 25-1/2 inches (81.3 x 64.8 cm)
Signed upper left: *Koyanagui*

Estimate: $2,500-$3,500

64049

ITALIAN SCHOOL (16th Century)
Dormant Ariadne
Pen and sepia ink on paper laid on two additional sheets
7-1/2 x 9-1/4 inches (19.1 x 23.5 cm)

PROVENANCE:
Dr. George La Porte;
Jan Nicolaas Streep;
Raydon Gallery, New York (label mat verso);
Private collection, New York.

EXHIBITED:
Arkansas Art Center, Little Rock, 1980 (label mat verso).

Estimate: $500-$1,000

64050

Circle of CHRISTOPH SCHWARZ (German, 1545-1592)
The Coronation of the Virgin
Pen, ink, and wash on beige paper mounted to second sheet
10-1/4 x 7 inches (26.0 x 17.8 cm)

PROVENANCE;
Dr. Hans Tauber, Graz;
Edouardo Cecionesi, Genoa;
Private collection, New York.

Estimate: $800-$1,200

64051

ITALIAN SCHOOL (17th/18th Century)
Temptation of Christ
Brown ink and wash on laid buff paper mounted to a second sheet
9 x 8-3/4 inches (22.9 x 22.2 cm)
Unidentified collector's stamp in lower right corner

PROVENANCE:
Chevalier d'Henin, 1785;
Chevalier Felix Emile d'Henin, 1815;
Chevalier Michele d'Henin;
Private collection, New York.

Estimate: $500-$700

64052

Attributed to DOMENICO CRESTI (Italian, 1559-1638)
Mars, Mercury, and Minerva
Brown ink and wash heightened with white chalk on grey paper laid on two sheets of paper
Sheet: 7 x 6-3/4 inches (17.8 x 17.1 cm); image: 6-1/2 x 6-1/2 inches
Signed lower right by a later hand: *Julio Rom__*

PROVENANCE:
Jan Nicolaas Streep;
Gustav Nooteboom;
Private collection, New York.

Estimate: $1,000-$1,500

64053 - no lot

64054

Attributed to PALAMEDES PALAMEDESZ
(Dutch, 1607-1638)
Military Procession
Pen, ink, and wash on paper laid on a second sheet
2-1/2 x 5-1/2 inches (6.4 x 14.0 cm)

Estimate: $800-$1,200

64055

After FERDINAND BOL (Dutch, 1616-1680)
David Taking Leave of Jonathan (Samuel 20: 41-42), 19th century
Pen and ink and brown wash on paper
7-1/2 x 5-1/2 inches (19.1 x 14.0 cm)
Compare with the work in the Louvre, Paris (22.995).

PROVENANCE:
Jan Nicolaas Streep

Estimate: $500-$700

64056

JAN VAN NOORDT (Dutch, circa 1620-after 1676)
Coastal Landscape, 1688
Ink wash on buff paper
Sheet: 16-1/2 x 12 inches (41.9 x 30.5 cm); image: 10 1/2 x 7 3/4 inches
Initialed and dated lower center: *J.V.N. 1688*

PROVENANCE:
Jan Nicolaas Streep;
Private collection, New York.

Estimate: $1,000-$1,500

64057

Manner of BARENT FABRITIUS (Dutch, 1624-1673)
A Noble Outing
Graphite, brown ink, and wash on buff paper
13-1/4 x 10 inches (33.7 x 25.4 cm)

PROVENANCE:
Jan Nicolaas Streep;
Gustav Nooteboom;
Private collection, New York.

An attribution to Nicolaes Maes (Dutch, 1634-1693) has also been
suggested.

Estimate: $800-$1,200

64058

FLEMISH SCHOOL (17th/18th Century)
Portrait of a Man (Peter the Great?)
Charcoal and white chalk on blue paper
12-1/4 x 8-3/4 inches (31.1 x 22.2 cm)

PROVENANCE:
Chevalier d'Henin;
Chevalier Emile Felix d'Henin;
Chevalier Emile d'Henin;
Private collection, New York.

Estimate: $800-$1,200

64059

Attributed to GODFRIED MAES (Flemish, 1649-1700)
The Holy Family
Pen and brown wash on paper partially laid on a second sheet
7-1/2 x 5-3/4 inches (19.1 x 14.6 cm)
Inscribed by a later hand on verso of primary sheet: *Godfroy Maes, born at
Antwerp in 1660, was a Scholar of / his Father, was so early in Life as 1682
chosen Director / of the Academy in that City; the time of his Death is / not
mentioned.*

Estimate: $1,500-$2,500

64060

School of GERARD DE LAIRESSE (Flemish, 1641-1711)
Pomona and Hippocrates
Sepia ink and grey wash on paper laid on a second sheet
Sheet: 9-3/4 x 8 inches (24.8 x 20.3 cm); image: 9-1/4 x 7-1/2 inches (33.5 x 19.1 cm)

PROVENANCE:
Jan Nicolaas Streep;
Private collection, New York.

Estimate: $600-$800

64061

Circle of EUSTACHE LE SUEUR (French, 1616-1655)
Mystical Vision of a Saint
Ink and brown wash on buff laid paper affixed in the corners to a second sheet
Sheet: 15-1/2 x 13 inches (39.4 x 33.0 cm); image: 11-3/4 x 8 inches (29.8 x 20.3 cm)

PROVENANCE:
Edouardo Cecionesi, Genoa;
Dr. Hans Tauber, Graz;
Private collection, New York.

Estimate: $400-$600

64062

VENETIAN SCHOOL (18th Century)
Saint Theresa, a second female saint and Charity (possibly preliminary study for an altarpiece)
Brush point and ink wash over charcoal on buff paper laid on second sheet
9-1/2 x 6-1/4 inches (24.1 x 15.9 cm)

PROVENANCE:
Chevalier d'Henin, 1785;
Chevalier Emile Felix d'Henin, 1815;
Chevalier Michele d'Henin, 1877 (Lugt 248);
Private collection, New York.

Estimate: $1,000-$1,500

64063 - no lot

64064

Attributed to GIROLAMO BONINI (Italian, 1620-1690)
Two Religious Scenes, possibly studies for altarpieces
Pen and ink and wash on toned paper

Christ Giving Communion to the Apostles (Last Supper)
Pen and ink and sepia wash with oxydized white heightening on toned paper laid on second paper
12-3/4 x 9-3/4 inches (32.4 x 24.8 cm)
Squared with graphite lines

Lucas Medicus, Salutat Vos, Col. IV.14 (per inscription in margin of drawing)
Pen and ink and brown wash with oxydized white heightening on toned paper
11-3/4 x 7-1/8 inches (29.8 x 17.8 cm)

Estimate: $1,200-$1,500

64065 - no lot

64066

ITALIAN SCHOOL (17th Century)
*The Wedding at Cana and Mary
Magdalene Washing Christ's Feet
(Bearded Head* verso)
Graphite, brown pen, and ink on paper
11-1/2 x 18 inches (29.2 x 45.7 cm)
Signed illegibly lower left: *Giu__*
Inscribed illegibly verso: *G__ Tander*

Estimate: $600-$800

64067

Circle of OTTAVIANO DANDINI (Italian, d. 1750)
Mythological Scene (recto) and *Figure Study* by
another hand (verso)
Black crayon on paper
Image recto: 8 x 11-3/4 inches (20.3 x 29.8 cm); image
verso: 11-3/4 x 8 inches (29.8 x 20.3 cm)

PROVENANCE:
Dr. George La Porte;
Jan Nicolaas Streep;
Private collection, New York.

Estimate: $800-$1,200

64068

Circle of GIOVANNI BATTISTA TIEPOLO (Italian, 1696-1770)
The Disputation
Ink and grey wash on laid paper
9-1/2 x 6-3/4 inches (24.1 x 17.1 cm)

PROVENANCE:
Frick Collection, New York (label mat verso);
Raydon Gallery, New York (label mat verso);
Private collection, New York.

EXHIBITED:
Arkansas Art Center, Little Rock, 1979 (exhibited as a Giovanni Battista Piazzetta (Italian, 1682-1754)).

Estimate: $4,000-$6,000

64069

Attributed to GIOVANNI DOMENICO TIEPOLO (Italian, 1727-1804)
Papal Declaration (St. Augustine with Scribe and Angels)
Pen and ink and brown wash on buff paper laid on a second sheet
Sheet: 15 x 10-1/2 inches (38.1 x 26.7 cm); image: 9 x 8 inches

PROVENANCE:
Chevalier d'Henin;
Chevalier Emile Felix d'Henin;
Chevalier Michele d'Henin;
Private collection, New York.

Estimate: $6,000-$9,000

64070

ITALIAN SCHOOL (Late 17th Century)
Capriccio
Oil and brown wash on paper laid on a second
sheet
12 x 14-1/2 inches (30.5 x 36.8 cm)

PROVENANCE:
Chevalier d'Henin, Venice, 1785;
Chevalier Emile Felix d'Henin, 1818;
Chevalier Michele d'Henin, 1877;
Private collection, New York.

Featured in the drawing are several famous Roman
monuments: the Tomb of Augustus (right), San
Giovanni in Laterano (center), and the Basilica of
Maxentius (left).

Estimate: $1,000-$1,500

64071

VENETIAN SCHOOL (Italian, 18th Century)
Coat of Arms, possibly Charles V
Pen and sepia ink on buff paper laid onto a second
sheet
3-3/4 x 4-3/4 inches (9.5 x 12.1 cm)

PROVENANCE:
Chevalier d'Henin, Venice;
Chevalier F. E. d'Henin;
Chevalier Michele d'Henin;
Private collection, New York.

Estimate: $400-$600

64072

WOLFGANG JACOB GERSTENS (German, circa 1730-circa 1760)
Sculptural Studies for Niches: Venus and Cupid, Minerva, circa 1760
Wash and ink on buff laid paper hinged to a second sheet
Sheet: 7-1/2 x 9 inches (19.1 x 22.9 cm); image: 7 x 8 1/4 inches
Inscribed on the second sheet: *N7i / Wolfgang Jacob Gerstens / bildforum / in München, Schleissheim / und Nymphenburg / 1760 / 334*

PROVENANCE:
Dr. George La Porte;
Private collection, New York.

Estimate: $400-$600

64073

Attributed to JOSEPH ANTON KOCH (Austrian, 1768-1839)
Extensive Landscape with Figures
Pen, ink, and grey wash on buff paper
8 x 12-3/4 inches (20.3 x 32.4 cm)
Unidentified collector's stamp on verso

PROVENANCE:
Dr. George La Porte;
Jan Nicolaas Streep;
Gustav Nooteboom;
Private collection, New York.

Estimate: $2,000-$3,000

64074

ANTHONY VANDYKE COPLEY FIELDING (British, 1787-1855)
Loch Awe, Scotland
Watercolor and pencil on paper
13 x 9 inches (33.0 x 22.9 cm)

PROVENANCE:
Jeremy North Gallery, Thomasboro Crossroads, North Carolina (label verso);
Private collection.

Copley Fielding, one of the greatest masters of 19th-century British watercolor painting, produced this view of Loch Awe in the manner of a stage set displaying the drama of the lake framed by mountains. With a gentle reductive palette of ochres, sepias, yellows, and blues, the artist placed a young family as well as a herd of cattle in the foreground to establish relative scale for the grandeur of this natural spectacle before them. The artist sketched the figures, animals, and most important outlines of the mountains in graphite, using them as guidelines for his colored washes. Located in Argyll and Bute, Loch Awe is renowned for its trout fishing and for a number of ruined castles, including Kilchurn Castle. The powerful Clan Campbell had its origins in the region of Loch Awe, the third largest freshwater loch in Scotland.

Estimate: $1,000-$1,500

64075

School of FRANÇOIS BOUCHER (French, 1703-1770)
Putti in Flight
Red chalk on buff laid paper mounted on cardboard
9 x 9 inches (22.9 x 22.9 cm)
Signed lower right by a later hand

PROVENANCE:
Chevalier Michel d'Henin;
Raydon Gallery, New York;
Private collection, New York.

EXHIBITED:
Arkansas Art Center, Little Rock, 1979 (label mat verso).

Estimate: $1,500-$2,500

64076

School of HUBERT ROBERT (French, 1733-1808)
Roman Ruins with Figures
Graphite, brown ink, and wash on buff paper laid on cardboard
5-3/4 x 8 inches (14.6 x 20.3 cm)

PROVENANCE:
Chevalier d'Henin, Venice, 1785;
Chevalier Emile Felix d'Henin, 1815;
Chevalier Michele d'Henin, 1877;
Private collection, New York.

Estimate: $1,000-$2,000

64077

Attributed to JEAN SIMON BERTHÉLEMY (French, 1743-1811)
Villa Borghese
Red crayon on laid paper mounted on a second sheet
Sheet: 14-1/2 x 20 inches (36.8 x 50.8 cm); image: 10-3/4 x 17-3/4 inches

PROVENANCE:
Dr. George La Porte;
Private collection, New York.

An attribution to Hubert Robert (French, 1733-1808) has also been suggested.

Estimate: $1,500-$2,000

64078 - no lot

64079

Attributed to PIERRE-PAUL PRUD'HON (French, 1758-1823)

Odalisque (Potiphar's Wife)
Graphite and chalk on blue paper affixed along edges to a window mat
Paper mat: 9 x 10-3/4 inches (22.9 x 27.3 cm); image: 5-1/2 x 7 inches

PROVENANCE:
Paul Bronde;
Private collection, New York.

Estimate: $2,000-$3,000

64080

Attributed to JEAN-BAPTISTE ISABEY (French, 1767-1855)

Young Smoker in an Ornate Costume
Black and white chalk and bistre wash on buff paper laid on a second sheet
Sheet: 13 x 10 inches (33.0 x 25.4 cm); image: 10-3/4 x 8-1/2 inches (27.3 x 21.6 cm)

Estimate: $2,500-$3,500

64081

CHRISTOPHE GEORGE MATTHES (German, 1738-1805) and CONTINENTAL SCHOOL (18th Century)
Figural Compositions (4)

(Matthes) *Portrait of a Woman*, 1805
Charcoal on paper
Sheet: 21 x 16-1/2 inches (53.3 x 41.9 cm); image: 18-1/2 x 14-3/4 inches (47 x 37.5 cm)
Signed lower right: *C.G.L. Matthes del 1805*

(Matthes) *Portrait of a Boy*, 1798
Charcoal on paper
26-1/2 x 20 inches (67.3 x 50.8 cm)
Signed and dated lower left: *CGL Matthes / 22nd Aug. 1798*

(Continental School) *Mythological Figures (Perseus and Andromeda)*
Charcoal heightened with white chalk on grey paper
21-1/2 x 24-1/2 inches (54.6 x 62.2 cm)

(Continental School) *Mythological Figures (Woman with Mirror and Winged Man)*, 1777
Charcoal heightened with white chalk on grey paper
21-1/2 x 24-1/2 inches (54.6 x 62.2 cm)
Signed illegibly and dated in shadow beneath woman's right hand: ___ *1777*

Estimate: $1,200-$1,800

64082

MENO MUHLIG (Swiss, 1823-1873) and CHRISTIAN GOTTLIEB GEISSLER (German, 1729-1814)
Wilhelm Tell? (*Swiss Patriots in a Forest Hideout*), circa 1860; and *Abraham and the Angel*, 1787 (two drawings)

(Muhlig) Graphite and silverpoint on card
11-1/2 x 8-3/4 inches (29.2 x 22.2 cm)
Signed lower right: *Meno Muhlig*

(Geissler) Watercolor on paper
8-3/4x 7 inches (image) (22.2 x 17.5 cm)
Signed and dated lower right: *Geissler f. d. 18 Oct / 1787*
Additional faint inscription in lower left

PROVENANCE:
(Muhlig) Dr. Oscar Costa.
(Geissler) Dr. George La Porte.

Estimate: $500-$1,000

64083

FRANÇOIS LÉON BENOUVILLE (French, 1821-1859)
Saint Claire Mourning the Body of Saint Francis of Assisi, circa 1854-55
Graphite on rice paper laid on a second sheet
8-1/4 x 10-1/4 inches (21.0 x 26.0 cm)
Artist's stamp in lower right

This drawing is very likely a preliminary compositional study for a painting in the Conde Museum of the Chateau de Chantilly.

Estimate: $1,000-$2,000

64084

Attributed to GIACOMO GUARDI (Italian, 1764-1835)
S. Geremia, Venice
Pen and ink wash on paper affixed along edges to window mat
7 x 10 inches (17.8 x 25.4 cm)

PROVENANCE:
Chevalier d'Henin;
Chevalier Michel d'Henin;
Dr. George La Porte;
Private collection, New York.

Estimate: $3,000-$4,000

64085

FRITZ L'ALLEMAND (German-Austrian, 1812-1866) and SCHOOL OF PIETRO LONGHI (Italian, 1702-1785)
Four Military Studies, 1866 and *Portrait of a Man* (two drawings)
Graphite on paper and chalks on paper, respectively
12-3/4 x 10 inches (32.4 x 25.4 cm) and
Signed and dated lower right: *Fritz L'Allemand / 1866*

PROVENANCE (L'Allemand):
Georges and Marianne Kuhner, Vienna and Los Angeles;
Private collection, New York.

PROVENANCE (School of Longhi):
Collector's stamp lower left.

Estimate: $500-$700

64086

FRIEDRICH GIESSMANN (German, 1810-1847) and JEAN-LOUIS DEMARNE (French, 1744-1829)
Two Landscape Drawings

(Giessmann) *Wooded Landscape* (2-sided sheet)
Pen and ink on paper
5 x 7 inches (12.7 x 17.8 cm)
Signed in ink lower left: *F. GEISMAN*

(Demarne) *Wooded Landscape with Figures and Cattle*
Brush point and ink wash on paper laid down on rag board
18-1/2 x 13 inches (47 x 33 cm)

PROVENANCE:
(Giessmann) Dr. George LaPorte;
Private collection, New York.

PROVENANCE:
(Demarne) Dr. George La Porte;
Private collection, New York.

Estimate: $1,200-$1,500

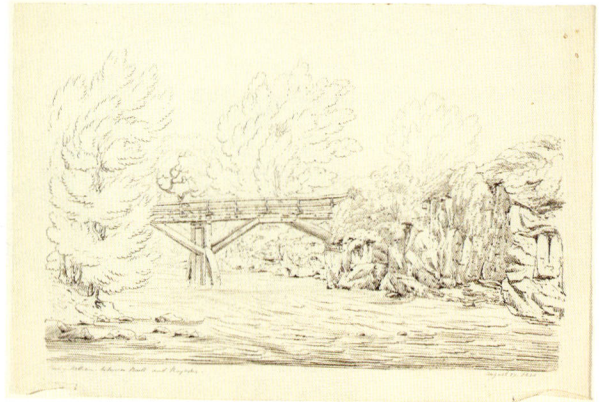

64087

ENGLISH SCHOOL (Early 19th Century)
Two Graphite Drawings

Land about the Mogen Head, S. W. Coast of Ireland, 1826
Graphite on paper
4-1/4 x 12 inches (10.8 x 30.5 cm)
Dated and inscribed lower right: *Land about the Mogen Head / S. W. Coast of Ireland. / on board H. M. S. Magnet - 5 miles from shore / June 20th 1826*

Pont y Kithon between Built and Rayader, 1820
Graphite on paper
Sheet: 9 x 13-1/2 inches; image:7-3/4 x 12 inches (47 x 33 cm)
Inscribed and dated lower left and right: *Pont y Kithon between Built and Rayader / August 17,1820*

Estimate: $500-$700

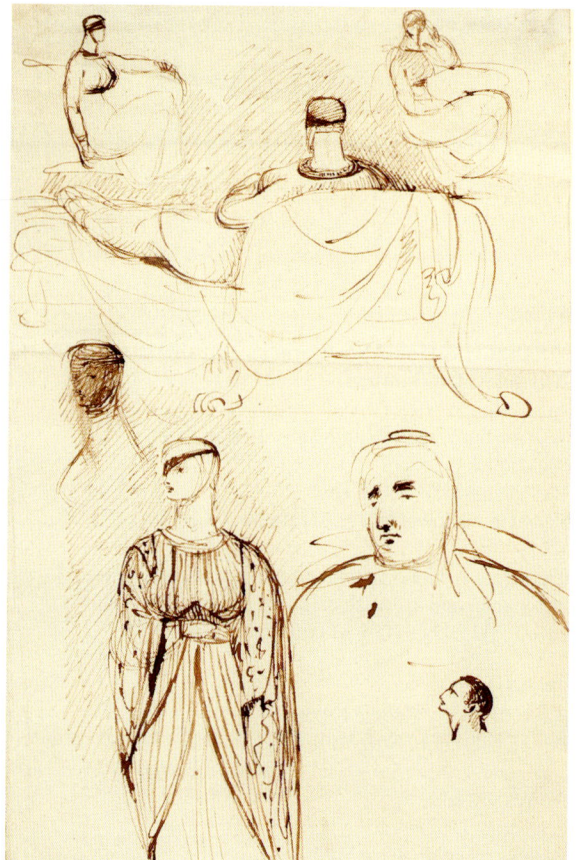

64088

BENJAMIN ROBERT HAYDON (British, 1786-1846)
Figure Studies
Pen and brown ink on paper
12-1/2 x 8 inches (31.8 x 20.3 cm)

PROVENANCE:
Baskin collection, Northampton, Massachusetts;
Frederick Cummings, 1973;
Private collection, New York.

Estimate: $600-$900

64089

Attributed to EDWARD LEAR (British, 1812-1888)
Two Middle Eastern Landscapes

Coastal Landscape
Pen and ink wash on brown paper
12 x 19 inches (30.5 x 48.3 cm)
Partial trimmed signature in lower right

In the Hills
Charcoal, pen, and ink wash heightened with white wash on brown paper laid on a second sheet
11 x 16-1/2 inches (27.9 x 41.9 cm)

Estimate: $2,000-$3,000

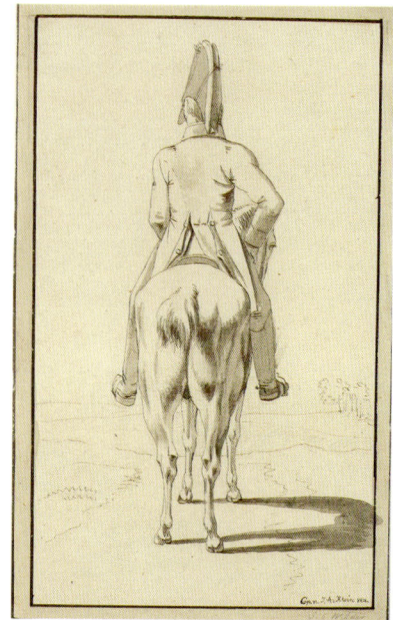

64090

CESARE DELL'ACQUA (Italian, 1821-1904) and G. C. WILDER (English, early 19th century)
Two Drawings of Military Subjects

(Dell'Acqua) *Equestrian, Military and Character Studies*, 1846
Watercolor and graphite on paper
7-1/2 x 10 inches (19.1 x 25.4 cm)
Signed, dated, and inscribed lower right: *Cesare Dell'Acqua inv. / 46*

(Wilder) *Captain J. A. Klein*, 1814
Pen, ink, and wash on paper with border
7-1/4 x 4-3/4 inches (18.4 x 12.1 cm)
Signed, dated, and inscribed lower right corner: *Cap.n. J. A. Klein 1814 / J. C. Wilder*

Estimate: $3,000-$5,000

64091

FERDINAND FELLNER (German, 1799-1859)
Heraldic Allegory or Study for Ludwig II Mausoleum
Grey ink, pen, and wash on off-white wove paper
12-1/4 x 14-1/2 inches (31.1 x 36.8 cm)
Ink stamp verso inscribed in circle: *SG*
Inscribed left and right with names and countries of the two royal German houses

PROVENANCE:
Wolfgang Gurlitt, Munich.

LITERATURE AND EXHIBITION:
"German Master drawings of the Nineteenth Century," Busch-Reisinger Museum, Harvard University, Cambridge, Massachusetts, 1972, cat. no. 17.

Estimate: $1,500-$2,000

64092

Attributed to KAREL FERDINAND VENNEMAN (Belgian, 1802-1875)
The Village Doctor
Watercolor and gouache on paper
6 x 5 inches (15.2 x 12.7 cm)
Possible abraded signature lower left

PROVENANCE:
Dr. Oscar K. Cosla, New York;
Jan Nicolaas Streep;
Private collection, New York.

Estimate: $300-$500

64093

SWEDISH SCHOOL (19th Century)
Portrait of a Seated Woman, 1847
Black and white chalk on brown paper
9-3/4 x 8-1/4 inches (24.8 x 21.0 cm)
Signed illegibly and dated lower left: *L. F. __bsjohn. Sept. 1847.*

PROVENANCE:
Dr. George La Porte;
Jan Nicolaas Streep;
Gustav Nooteboom;
Private collection, New York.

Estimate: $400-$600

64094

FRIEDRICH VON AMERLING (Austrian, 1803-1887)
Head of a Young Bearded Venetian Man in Profile, 1860
Watercolor and chalks on paper
19 x 12-3/4 inches (48.3 x 32.5 cm)
Vestige of name or title in faded ink upper left
Inscribed verso: *Venedig, April 1860*

Estimate: $2,000-$3,000

64095

ANDERS LEONARD ZORN (Swedish, 1860-1920)
Portrait of a Man Reading in a Den, circa 1890
Pen and ink on paper laid on paperboard
8-1/4 x 4-3/4 inches (21.0 x 12.1 cm)

PROVENANCE:
possibly Chester Dale collection;
Private collection, New York.

Estimate: $4,000-$6,000

64096

MARC CHAGALL (Belorussian, 1887-1985)
Four Etchings from Les Âmes Mortes, 1948
Etching
From the edition of 368

Le troika s'est renversée
9 x 11-3/4 inches (22.9 x 29.8 cm)

Man with a Pipe
11-1/4 x 8-3/4 inches (28.6 x 22.2 cm)
Signed in the plate lower right: *Marc Chagall*

Sobakevitsch
11 x 8-1/4 inches (27.9 x 21 cm)
Signed in the plate lower right: *M. Chagall*

Le traktir
8-3/4 x 11-1/4 inches 22.2 x 28.6 cm)

Estimate: $1,200-$1,500

64097

JOSÉ BORRÁS SOLANA (Spanish, 1857-1947)
Peasants Sitting at Tables
Black ink over graphite on buff card
Image: 7-1/2 x 11-1/8 inches (19.1 x 28.3 cm)
Sheet: 12-1/2 x 16 inches (31.8 x 40.6 cm)
Signed in ink lower left: *J. Solana*

PROVENANCE:
Private collection, New York.

Estimate: $22,000-$28,000

64098

EDMUND DARCH LEWIS (American, 1835-1910)
A View of Cuba, 1874
Oil on canvas
22-1/4 x 36 inches (56.5 x 91.4 cm)
Signed and dated lower right: *Edmund D. Lewis 1874*

Estimate: $25,000-$35,000

64099

ARTHUR PARTON (American, 1842-1914)
Pair of Berkshire Landscapes, 1872
Oil on canvas
34-1/4 x 40-1/4 inches (87.0 x 102.2 cm) each
One of the pair (scene with large haystack on right) signed and dated lower right: *Arthur Parton 1872*

Estimate: $15,000-$25,000

64100

DAVID JOHNSON (American, 1827-1908)
The Children's Playground, 1873
Oil on canvas
13-1/2 x 21-1/8 inches (34.3 x 53.7 cm)
Signed, titled, and dated verso: *"The Children's Play Ground" at Dashville / Ulster Co.N.Y. / David Johnson / 1873*

Nailed to back of the new stretcher bar is the length of Johnson's original stretcher bar bearing his original inscription: *The Children's Playground at / Dashville. Ulster Co. / N.Y. / David Johnson. 1873.*

PROVENANCE:
Knoedler-Modarco Galleries, New York (label verso);
Maxwell Galleries, San Francisco, California (label verso).

LITERATURE:
Gwendolyn Owens, "Nature Transcribed. The Landscapes and Still Lifes of David Johnson (1827-1908)," exh. cat., Herbert F. Johnson Museum of Art, 1988, listed in checklist, p. 71 (photo at Knoedler Galleries).

Estimate: $12,000-$16,000

64101

ALFRED JACOB MILLER (American, 1810-1874)
Portrait of a Fur Trapper
Oil on canvas
22-1/4 x 27-1/4 inches (56.5 x 69.2 cm)
Signed lower right: *A.J. Miller, P.*

Estimate: $15,000-$25,000

64102

FROM THE FLANNER & BUCHANAN CORPORATE COLLECTION

VICTOR DE GRAILLY (French, 1804-1889)
Niagara Falls, circa 1850
Oil on canvas
17 x 23-1/2 inches (43.2 x 59.7 cm)
Signed lower center in the shadow of a boulder: *Grailly* or *Chailly*

PROVENANCE:
Vose Galleries, Boston.

The author of this remarkable view of Niagara Falls, French artist Victor de Grailly, gained considerable popularity in the United States for his landscape paintings of American views. Although there is some speculation that de Grailly may have been in the United States from 1840 to 1870, there is no concrete evidence to support this as many of de Grailly's American landscapes were based on engravings from British artist-adventurer William Henry Bartlett's *American Scenery* series published in London in 1840.

Nevertheless, de Grailly's lively scenes found a ready audience in the United States, and his work was exhibited in locales as diverse as Charleston, South Carolina; Baltimore, Toronto; New York; Brooklyn; Albany; and Sandusky, Ohio. In 1854, a number of his paintings were auctioned in Portland, Maine.

De Grailly was born in Paris and began his art studies under Jean Victor Bertin, a neo-classical landscape painter who also taught Jean-Baptiste Camille Corot. De Grailly first exhibited at the Paris Salon in 1833, where he continued to show his paintings until 1880. He made copies of works by Claude Lorrain, but also painted original compositions of French, Italian, and British landscapes. His paintings can be found in important public collections including The White House, Baltimore Museum of Art, Brooklyn Museum of Art, Farnsworth Museum of Art, Portland Museum of Art, New-York Historical Society, and the West Point Museum.

This lot is accompanied by a richly-informative letter from 19th-century American landscape specialist, Dr. Michael Quick. In it he endorses the attribution to de Grailly on the basis of photographs, identifies the artist's specific vantage point on the falls, and makes careful note of the specific formal qualities of the painting which are characteristic of de Grailly's style.

As Dr. Quick notes, in part: "The view is from Goat Island on the American side, with the Upper Falls in the foreground, including atop the falls a boardwalk that led to a tower, and then the great horseshoe beyond it and the great sweep of the Canadian (then English) Falls in the distance, with the Canadian bank of the Niagara River in the far distance. The foreground is enlivened by a group of picnickers on the sloping grass at the left, and a couple strolling down the path at the right. There are goats near both groups, and banks of mature foliage rising beyond them at both the left and the right.

Like many or all of de Grailly's American subjects, this painting was based on an early engraving, specifically the published engraving, *Niagara Falls*, by William James Bennett from the 1830s. The painting followed the engraving quite closely, although the painter added the promenading couple on the descending path, which he enlarged, and he updated the Bennett image by adding the Terrapin Tower (1829-1870), which he may have seen in the Daguerreotypes that were widely available in the 1850's. It is characteristic of de Grailly to enlarge the path in order to create movement into depth. Also typical of the painter is the way he enlarged the distant foliage groups in the distance in order to create a deeper far distance. Entirely typical of the artist are his addition of the bulky cumulus clouds. Thus he has added considerably greater form in the distance, with the enhanced tree groups and the bank of clouds, both with the objective of increasing the prominence and depth of the distance. This stress upon a very deep distance is part of de Grailly's style.

Both the range of colors and the range of their intensity are entirely characteristic of de Grailly, including the addition of the color associated with sunset. To my eye, everything about the way that this landscape was painted it characteristic of the artist's style. It is my considered and definite opinion that this painting, *Niagara Falls*, is the work of Victor de Grailly, without any doubt."

Estimate: $6,000-$9,000

64103

WILLIAM SANFORD MASON (American, 1824-1864)
The Flower Gatherers and *The Berry Pickers* [a pair], 1861
Oil on canvas
10 x 8-1/2 inches (25.4 x 21.6 cm)
Each signed and dated lower right: *W. Sanford Mason / 1861*

PROVENANCE:
Hirschl & Adler Galleries, Inc., New York, (labels verso);
Mrs. Virginia Cramer, purchased from the above.

LITERATURE:
The Magazine Antiques, June 1998, p. 767, ill in color, full-page ad.

Estimate: $5,000-$8,000

64104

ENOCH WOOD PERRY (American, 1831-1915)
Country Festival, 1865
Oil on canvas
17 x 30-3/4 inches (43.2 x 78.1 cm)
Signed and dated lower left: *E. Wood Perry 1865*

PROVENANCE:
Raydon Gallery, New York (label verso);
Private collection, New York.

EXHIBITED:
Danforth Museum, Framingham, Massachusetts, "The Düsseldorf Connection," 8-11-1982.

Estimate: $4,000-$6,000

64105

ENOCH WOOD PERRY (American, 1831-1915)
Girl Peeling Fruit Before a Fire
Oil on wood panel
20-1/2 x 24 inches (52.1 x 61.0 cm)

Estimate: $15,000-$20,000

64106

PROPERTY FROM A PRIVATE TEXAS
COLLECTION

HUDSON RIVER SCHOOL (19th Century)
Cecilia Metello's Tomb
Oil on canvas
18 x 24 inches (45.7 x 61.0 cm)

PROVENANCE:
Ronald Bourgeault Antiques, Hampton, New
Hampshire;
Private collection, Washington, D.C., acquired
from the above, 1975;
Thence by descent to the present owner.

Estimate: $4,000-$6,000

64107

School of FRANK DUVENECK (American, 1848-1919)
Head of a Berber
Oil on canvas laid down on panel
26 x 21 inches (66.0 x 53.3 cm)

PROVENANCE:
Marie Sterner, Blecken, Munich;
Joseph Katz, Baltimore, Maryland;
Hirschl & Adler Galleries, Inc., New York (as Frank Duveneck);
The Metropolitan Museum of Art, New York, purchased from the above,
1958;
Hirschl & Adler Galleries, Inc., New York, 1966;
A.B. Closson, Jr., Cincinnati, Ohio; (as Frank Duveneck);
Mr. and Mrs. Charles A. Du Bois, Cincinnati, Ohio;
Trosby Galleries, Palm Beach, Florida, 1966; (as Frank Duveneck);
Mrs. William E. Roschen, New York;
Thence by descent to the present owner, Sheldon, South Carolina.

Estimate: $3,000-$5,000

64108

Attributed to THOMAS SULLY (American, 1783-1872)
The Hours
Oil on canvas
24 x 20 inches (61.0 x 50.8 cm)

PROVENANCE:
Mrs. Ruth E. Sherlock, Kingman, Arizona;
Sotheby Parke-Bernet, Los Angeles, June 6, 1978, lot 536;
Acquired by the present owner from the above.

LITERATURE:
E. Biddle and M. Fielding, *The Life and Works of Thomas Sully (1783-1872)*, Philadelphia, 1921, no. 2338 (probably).

Thomas Sully's *The Hours* is listed in the artist's register of his works, published in Edward Biddle and Mantle Fielding's *The Life and Works of Thomas Sully (1783-1872)*, as having been copied from an engraving by Samuel Shelley (1756-1808) with the same title. When the present owner purchased this painting from Sotheby Parke-Bernet, Los Angeles, in 1978, the lot was accompanied by a photograph of the inscription on the back of the painting prior to its relining that reads, "From Shelly / 1850 / 'The Hours' / Past, present and to-come." The photograph of the original inscription will be presented to the buyer of this lot.

A miniature composition on ivory painted by Samuel Shelley in 1801 titled "The Hours" and depicting this same subject is featured in the collection of the Metropolitan Museum of Art. As in Shelley's image of "The Hours," Sully's figures on the left and right represent "the past" and "to-come," while the central figure represents "the present." Sully noted in his register of works that the painting was begun February 19 and finished February 24, 1850 and was presented to his daughter, Ellen Sully.

Estimate: $12,000-$16,000

64109

MARTIN JOHNSON HEADE (American, 1819-1904)
Red Roses in a Silver Vase on Gold Velvet, circa 1885-1890
Oil on canvas
18 x 10 inches (45.7 x 25.4 cm)
Signed lower left: M.J. Heade

PROVENANCE:
Estate of Mrs. Edward G. Jenkins, Sr., Lyndon, Kentucky (granddaughter of Alvin Wood, Founder of Lyndon, Kentucky);
Private collection, Louisville, Kentucky, purchased from the above, circa 1975.

Dr. Stebbins's catalogue raisonné documents four floral still lifes which use the same decorative bud vase seen in the present painting as a container for presenting flowers (*The Life and Work of Martin Johnson Heade*, New Haven, 2000, cat. nos. 511, 512, 519 and 531). The vessel is a Japanese vase of the Meiji period. The body of the bottle is made of copper or brass, to which the silver bamboo decoration is applied.

The four other floral still lifes in which Heade depicted this Meiji vase are dated, or can be dated, according to Stebbins' scholarship, to the period between 1883 and 1890. In each of Heade's presentations of it, the vase is shown at the same angle that it is in the present work, with the applied decoration turned to the right, and at least half of it extending out of view around to the back of the vessel.

In c. 1865-75, more than a decade before he painted this group of still lifes, Heade made an oil sketch of the Japanese vase on a small 8 x 10 inch piece of unstretched canvas, now in the collection of the St. Augustine Historical Society, St. Augustine, FL (Stebbins, 2000, cat. no. 382). That study probably served as the "painted model" for this and the other related paintings. It is noteworthy to mention that the artist annotated his initial sketch of the Meiji vase with the words "on yellow table." The present painting indeed shows the vase on a yellow colored cloth, painted in Heade's characteristic way of showing the nap of velvet with many vertical strokes of the brushpoint.

The canvas containing Heade's initial annotated sketch of this vase also depicts a red rose that is not fully open and facing to the left. Other related oil sketches on small pieces of unstretched canvas from the same time frame also feature studies of red roses, probably painted from life to serve as models for later paintings (also in the St. Augustine Historical Society). (One of those small oil sketches depicts a rose very close in shape and profile to the large blossom Heade painted on the right side of this arrangement.) Interestingly, the pentimenti visible beneath the rose at top left in this bouquet reveal that Heade's original concept for this flower was shaped differently from its finished appearance. The pentimento is very close to the rose on the oil sketch containing his study for the vase. Taken together, it seems that this still life is more closely dependent upon Heade's initial sketches than the other four in the series with Meiji vases, which begin to deviate from the initial conception both in terms of kinds of tabletops they depict, and the extent to which rose leaves begin occluding parts of the vase. Consequently, the present still life may be the earliest, or one of the first, Heade created in the group of five.

We would like to thank Dr. Theodore E. Stebbins, Jr. for examining this work in the original and confirming its authenticity. This work will be included in the next edition of his Martin Johnson Heade catalogue raisonné.

A letter from Dr. Stebbins dated October 4, 2011 confirming the authenticity of the work and documenting it within the artist's *oeuvre* accompanies this lot.

Estimate: $40,000-$60,000

64110

OLIVER DENNETT GROVER (American, 1861-1927)
Italian Landscape with Moored Boats, 1914
Oil on canvas
9-1/2 x 13-1/2 inches (24.1 x 34.3 cm)
Signed and dated lower left: *Oliver Dennett Grover / 1914*

PROVENANCE:
Private collection, Ohio.

Estimate: $4,000-$6,000

64111

ANTHONY THIEME (American, 1888-1954)
Floral Garden, 1918
Watercolor on paper
9-1/4 x 14-1/4 inches (23.5 x 36.2 cm)
Signed and dated lower right: *AThieme / 1918*

Estimate: $800-$1,200

64112

JAMES ABBOTT MCNEILL WHISTLER (American, 1834-1903)
Fishing Boat (From the Second Venice Set), 1879-1880
Etching
6 x 9 inches (15.2 x 22.9 cm)

LITERATURE:
E.G. Kennedy, *The Etched Work of Whistler*, New York, 1910, no. 208.

Estimate: $8,000-$12,000

64113

ANTHONY THIEME (American, 1888-1954)
A View of Venice, 1922
Oil on board
12 x 20 inches (30.5 x 50.8 cm)
Signed and dated lower right: *AThieme / 1922*

Estimate: $3,000-$5,000

64114

PROPERTY OF AN EAST COAST INSTITUTION

CHILDE HASSAM (American, 1859-1935)
Oyster Sloop, Cos Cob, 1902
Oil on canvas
24 x 22 inches (61.0 x 55.9 cm)
Signed and dated lower left: *Childe Hassam 1902*

PROVENANCE:
The estate of the artist;
The American Academy of Arts and Letters, New York (deaccessioned);
The Frauwirth Family Art Trust, North Dartmouth, Massachusetts;
Acquired by the present owner from the above.

By the late nineteenth century, due largely to the efforts of artists John Twachtman (1853-1902) and J. Alden Weir (1852-1919), an art colony was established in Cos Cob, Connecticut, a modest waterfront section of Greenwich. With the completion of the railroad station in 1870, it took just eighty minutes-a mere thirty miles-to get to this hamlet. Cos Cob's popularity was bolstered by the *plein-air* instruction offered by both artists. The colony became a magnet for a wide spectrum of both professional and amateur painters.

Childe Hassam was a peripatetic artist, living and working up and down the Eastern seaboard and in Europe. He first visited Cos Cob in 1894, and returned periodically until 1917. The art colony attracted not only painters, but a wide variety of writers, editors, and musicians. Colonists gathered at the Holly House, a boarding house run by Josephine Lynne Holly and her daughter Constant. The admixture of "types" made for a lively bohemian atmosphere, and Hassam became a frequent guest and cherished member of the colony.

Although the artist previously favored garden images while painting in Appledore and on the Island of Shoals in New Hampshire, he turned his attention to more pedestrian subjects in Cos Cob. Inspired by the mills, barns, and shipyards-and the Holly House itself-Hassam's work in Cos Cob is a testament to his fascination with New England history. It is often also nostalgic, and the impact of industrialization become evident during the duration of Hassam's many visits.

If he stood on the porch of the Holly House, Hassam had an excellent view of the shipyard. From this vantage point, he painted a number of scenes of the oystermen that still insisted on using outdated sail powered craft that by this date and largely been replaced by steam boats. Hassam's trademark divided color and bravura brushwork are evident in this painting. Using a varied palette, the artist creates a sense of movement and vibrancy on the canvas.

Hassam's Cos Cob pictures make up an impressive part of his long and storied career working in New England.

References:
Deborah Epstein Solon, *Colonies of American Impressionism: Cos Cob, Old Lyme, Shinnecock and Laguna Beach* (Laguna Beach: Laguna Art Museum, 1999)
H. Barbara Weinberg, et. al., *Childe Hassam, American Impressionist* (Metropolitan Museum of Art: Yale University Press, 2004)

This work, illustrated in its original unrestored state, will be included in Stuart P. Feld's and Kathleen M. Burnside's forthcoming catalogue raisonné of the artist's works.

Estimate: $50,000-$70,000

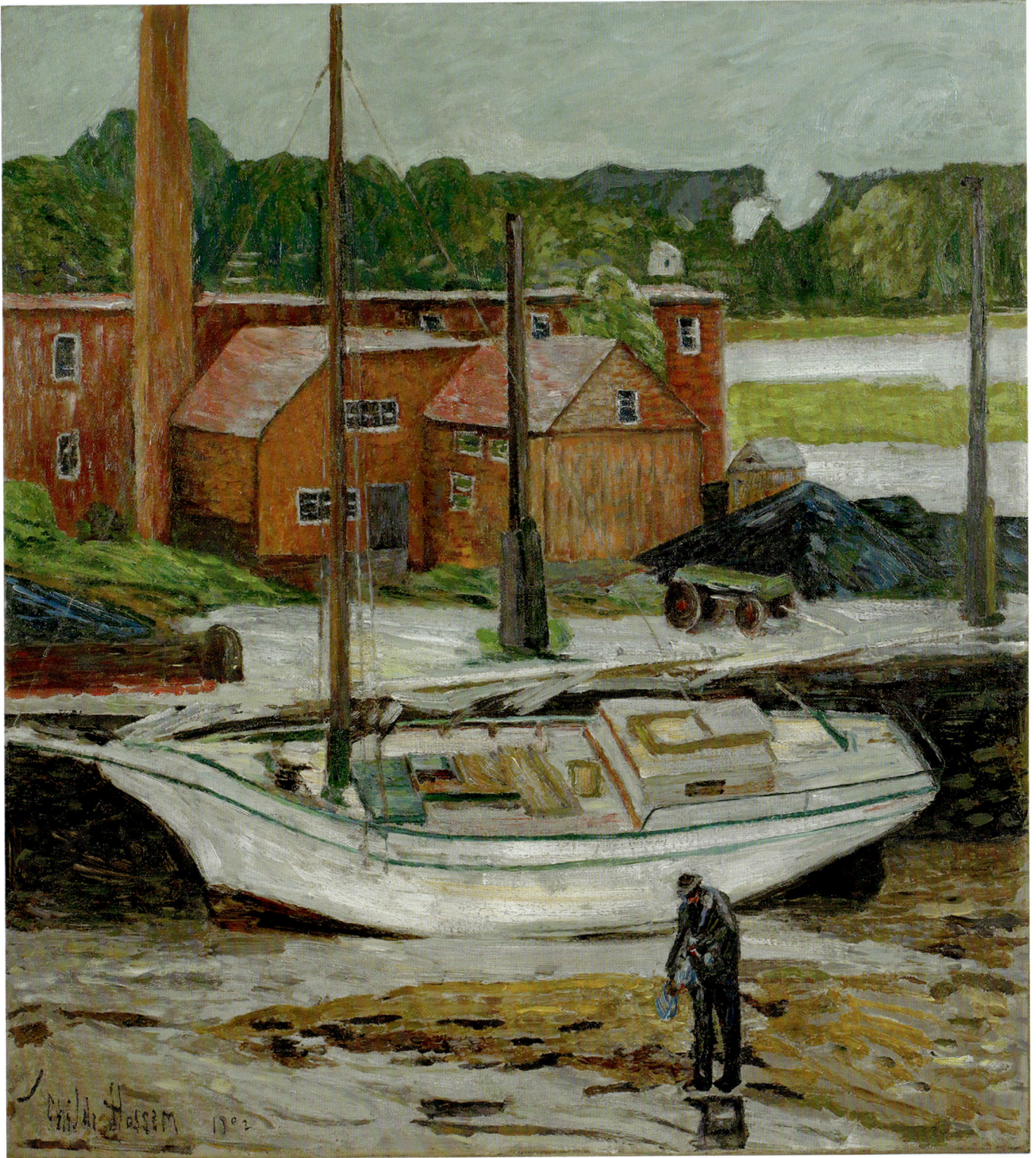

64115

PAUL CORNOYER (American, 1864-1923)
Set of Paintings from Washington Irving's "Rip Van Winkle" (4), circa 1896
Oil on board
10-3/4 x 20-3/4 inches (27.3 x 52.7 cm)
Each signed lower right: *Paul Cornoyer*

PROVENANCE:
The Southern Hotel, St. Louis, Missouri;
Mr. and Mrs. George Kilgen, St. Louis, Missouri;
By descent to the present owner, Roseville, California.

Best known for his poetic, Tonalist evocations of New York City, contemporary with the Ash Can School, Paul Cornoyer mastered a sense of place in his landscapes and cityscapes, wherever he was living. He honed his artistic talent during the 1890s in his native St. Louis, at the School of Fine Arts, and in Paris, at the Académie Julian, studying with Jules Lefebvre, Benjamin Constant, and Louis Blanc. His early streetscapes captured the hustle and bustle of a burgeoning St. Louis, most notably a mural cycle depicting the birth of the city, which he designed for the local Planters Hotel. Presaging his move to New York in 1899, this whimsical group of four paintings illustrating scenes from New Yorker Washington Irving's *Rip Van Winkle* was believed to have hung at another important St. Louis hotel, The Southern. With his trademark loose brushwork and moody palette, Cornoyer here sequentially interprets the famous story of the New York colonist Rip Van Winkle, who, seeking solace from his hen-pecking wife, wanders into the Kaatskill Mountains, drinks from the keg of some curious Dutchmen playing nine-pins, and awakens decades later, to return to a post-Revolution village no longer under British rule.

Estimate: $10,000-$15,000

64116

FRANK VINCENT DUMOND (American, 1865-1951)
Monastic Life, circa 1891
Oil on canvas
64-1/2 x 80 inches (163.8 x 203.2 cm)
Signed lower left: *F. V. Dumond*

EXHIBITED:
National Academy of Design, New York, 1892, no. 49;
World's Columbian Exposition, Chicago, 1893, no. 371.

This ambitious salon painting was one of five canvases Frank Vincent Dumond exhibited at the 1893 World's Columbian Exposition in Chicago. Together with the four other canvases he showed to great public acclaim, Monastic Life, the most celebrated of the group with its magical effect of light filtering through the trees, was a work Dumond painted in France shortly before his return to the United States in 1892. It is indebted to the work of the Symbolist painters Dumond intensely admired in the early phase of his career. Owing to its popularity at the World's Fair, *Monastic Life* was issued in a limited edition color print in 1896.

The lifesize cartoon for this painting (preparatory drawing in ink at the same scale as the painting, 64.4 x 80 inches) sold at Christie's East, New York, on February 14, 1990, lot 63.

In his own time, Dumond was often acknowledged as the most famous art instructor in the United States. He served on the faculty of the Art Students' League in New York for nearly 60 years, and taught many future luminaries of American Modernism including Georgia O'Keeffe and John Marin.

Estimate: $15,000-$20,000

64117

J. CHARLES ARTER (American, 1860-1923)
The Hay Gatherer
Oil on canvas
23-1/2 x 28-3/4 inches (59.7 x 73.0 cm)
Signed lower left: *J.C. Arter*

Estimate: $2,000-$3,000

64118

WILLARD LEROY METCALF (American, 1858-1925)
Woman in a Field, 1878
Oil on canvas
14 x 17 inches (35.6 x 43.2 cm)
Signed and dated lower left: *W. L. Metcalf 1878*

PROVENANCE:
Berry-Hill Galleries, New York, 1970s;
Mrs. Cramer, Virginia Purchased from the above in 1978;
Private collection.

This early work by Metcalf predates his period of study in France. It is similar in handling to his 1877 painting on board entitled "Cloudy Day, York Beach" (6-1/4 x 10-1/2 inches, collection of Molly Armstrong), reproduced in Elizabeth de Veer and Richard Boyle, *Sunlight and Shadow. The Life and Art of Willard Metcalf*, fig. 8.

This painting will be included in the forthcoming catalogue raisonne of the works of Willard L. Metcalf by Ira Spanierman and Richard J. Boyle.

Estimate: $40,000-$60,000

64119

PROPERTY FROM A PRIVATE COLLECTION, SAN DIEGO

DANIEL RIDGWAY KNIGHT (American, 1839-1924)
Young Woman Knitting
Oil on canvas
33 x 26 inches (83.8 x 66.0 cm)
Signed and inscribed lower left: *Ridgway Knight / Paris*

PROVENANCE:
Collection of Campbell H. Elkins, Lubbock, Texas;
Jerome H. Sharpe, San Diego, California, by bequest from the above.

Best known for his idyllic and picturesque scenes of rural peasant life, Daniel Ridgway Knight received critical acclaim, fame and success during his lifetime, and today his works are some of the most recognizable and beloved images in nineteenth century art. Often depicting young peasant women in pleasing landscapes much like the present work, Knight's works reflect the artist's optimism and admiration for the lives and work of the peasant class, as well as his eye for capturing the beauty of his natural surroundings.

Daniel Ridgway Knight was born in Philadelphia in 1839, and studied and exhibited at the Pennsylvania Academy of Fine Arts from 1858 to 1861, sharing classes with Thomas Eakins and Mary Cassatt. In 1861 the young artist sailed for France to study at the Ecole des Beaux-Arts, where he apprenticed with academic painters Charles Gleyre and Alexander Cabanel. Knight returned to Philadelphia in 1863 to enlist in the army during the Civil War, only to return to France in 1871 where he would reside for the remainder of his life.

Upon his return to France, Knight formed friendships with Pierre-Auguste Renoir, Alfred Sisley, and Alfred Wordsworth, and his work began to reflect the influence of the three great French Impressionists, with a keen attention to the effects of light during different times of day and a focus on everyday subjects. After meeting the artist Jean-Louis-Ernest Meissonier, he took residence in Poissy to be closer the renowned academic painter, who would have a tremendous influence on his work. Meissonier influenced Knight to incorporate a detailed style of realism in his compositions, and encouraged his artistic focus toward scenes of peasant life, which would become Knight's primary subject matter.

Often compared to his contemporary Jean-Francois Millet, Knight was strongly impressed by the artist's work, but in contrast with Millet and other painters among the emerging Realist movement in France, he set his focus on uplifting rather than fatalistic depictions of the rural class. Moving his attention away from the hardships of labor, Knight instead idealized his figures, rendering them in moments of contemplative rest or idle activity, or contently absorbed in performing the day's chores and set in colorful gardens or scenic riverside settings. These pleasing scenes of rural life proved highly popular among nineteenth century collectors both in France and abroad, and began to bring him the fortune and renown he would continue to enjoy.

From 1896, Knight established a home and studio outside Paris in Rolleboise, and drew his subjects and inspiration from the surrounding countryside. Knight not only painted the local people of Rolleboise, but also knew them personally and was an admired figure in the community. It was in Rolleboise that he began to paint scenes of his own garden overlooking the Seine, which would become his most sought after works.

Young Woman Knitting is an iconic example of the artist's work on a grand scale, painted with a masterful sense of composition and Impressionist technique. This work features the popular artist's most beloved subject matter, the young peasant woman idly absorbed in the French countryside, a subject proven to stand the test of time in its resonance with audiences from the Victorian era through the present.

Howard L. Rehs has confirmed the authenticity of this work and will include it in his forthcoming catalogue raisonné, which will be published by Rehs Galleries, Inc., www.ridgwayknight.com.

Estimate: $80,000-$120,000

PROPERTY FROM THE HOUSTON CLUB COLLECTION

The Houston Club is a member-owned private club that has been a gathering place for the city's business, financial, cultural, and civic leaders since it was established in 1894. Houston's oldest private club continues its tradition of excellence in an atmosphere steeped in history with a comfortable elegance that generations of Houstonians and Texans have come to expect. Heritage is pleased to be offering these two exceptional examples of Edmund Henry Osthaus' work that have prominently graced the foyer of the Houston Club for decades.

64120

PROPERTY FROM THE HOUSTON CLUB COLLECTION

EDMUND HENRY OSTHAUS (American, 1858-1928)
English Setter with Grouse
Oil on canvas
44 x 59 inches (111.8 x 149.9 cm)
Signed lower right: *Edmund Osthaus*

Estimate: $40,000-$60,000

64121

PROPERTY FROM THE HOUSTON CLUB COLLECTION

EDMUND HENRY OSTHAUS (American, 1858-1928)
English Setters in Field
Oil on canvas
39-1/2 x 49-1/2 inches (100.3 x 125.7 cm)
Signed lower right: *Edm H. Osthaus*

Estimate: $40,000-$60,000

64122

BIRGE HARRISON (American, 1854-1929)
Moonlit Landscape
Oil on canvas
18 x 22 inches (45.7 x 55.9 cm)
Signed lower left: *Birge Harrington*

Estimate: $6,000-$10,000

64123

ALDRO THOMPSON HIBBARD (American, 1886-1972)
Winter Light, 1912
Oil on canvas laid on board
8 x 10-1/2 inches (20.3 x 26.7 cm)
Signed and dated lower left: *A. T. Hibbard / 1912*

PROVENANCE:
Raydon Gallery, New York (label verso);
Private collection, New York.

EXHIBITED:
Museums at Sunrise, Charleston, West Virginia, "America's Best," July 1 – September 13, 1981 (label verso).

Estimate: $7,000-$9,000

64124

EMILE ALBERT GRUPPÉ (American, 1896-1978)
Winter Scene
Oil on canvas
31 x 32 inches (78.7 x 81.3 cm)
Signed lower right: *Emile A. Gruppé*

Estimate: $8,000-$12,000

64125

WILLIAM FRANCIS TAYLOR (American, 1883-1970)
Toward St. Agricole
Oil on canvas board
12 x 15-3/4 inches (30.5 x 40.0 cm)
Signed lower right: *W.F. Taylor*

Estimate: $4,000-$6,000

64126

EMILE ALBERT GRUPPÉ (American, 1896-1978)
The Blue Gate
Oil on canvas
26 x 30 inches (66.0 x 76.2 cm)
Signed lower right: *Emile A. Gruppé*
Inscribed on stretcher: *The Blue Gate by Emile A. Gruppé*

Estimate: $6,000-$9,000

64127

MARY LOUISE FAIRCHILD (American, 1866-1946)
Mont Saint Michel
Oil on canvas
24 x 30 inches (61.0 x 76.2 cm)
Signed lower left: *Mary Fairchild Low A.N.A.*
Inscribed on lower stretcher verso: *M.F. Low / Sagamore Road / Bronxville*

PROVENANCE:
The artist;
Private collection, by descent from the above;
Acquired by the present owner from the above, 2007.

Estimate: $6,000-$9,000

64128

HAYLEY R. LEVER (American, 1876-1958)
Gloucester Harbor, Massachusetts, 1918
Oil on canvas
15-1/2 x 19-1/2 inches (39.4 x 49.5 cm)
Signed and dated lower left: *Hayley Lever / 1918*

PROVENANCE:
Hirschl & Adler Galleries, Inc., (label verso);
Acquired by the present owner from the above, 1997.

Estimate: $4,000-$6,000

64129

WALTER KOENIGER (American, 1881-1943)
Winter Landscape
Oil on canvas
38 x 45 inches (96.5 x 114.3 cm)
Signed lower left: *W. Koeniger*

Estimate: $5,000-$7,000

64130

ERIC SLOANE (American, 1905-1985)
Barn on the Hillside
Oil on masonite
24-1/2 x 29 inches (62.2 x 73.7 cm)
Signed and inscribed lower right: *To Brass / Bugle / Eric Sloane*

PROVENANCE:
The artist;
Louise Mondani Graham, owner of The Brass Bugle Antiques, Warren, Connecticut;
Thence by descent to the present owner.

Estimate: $8,000-$12,000

64131

CHARLES ROLLO PETERS (American, 1862-1928)
Landscape with Windmill
Oil on canvas
18 x 23 inches (45.7 x 58.4 cm)
Signed lower right: *Charles Rollo Peters*

Estimate: $5,000-$7,000

64132

ALEXANDER A. DZIGURSKI (American, 1911-1995)
High Tide at Sunset
Oil on canvas
30 x 48 inches (76.2 x 121.9 cm)
Signed lower right: *A. DZIGURSKI*

Estimate: $3,000-$5,000

64133

EMILE ALBERT GRUPPÉ(American, 1896-1978)
Bass Rocks
Oil on canvas board
12 x 16 inches (30.5 x 40.6 cm)
Signed lower left: *Emile A. Gruppé*

Estimate: $2,000-$3,000

64134

OLIVER DENNETT GROVER (American, 1861-1927)
Storm over a Western Landscape, 1924
Oil on canvas laid on masonite
11-1/4 x 15-1/4 inches (28.6 x 38.7 cm)
Signed and dated lower left: *O. D. Grover 24*

PROVENANCE:
Private collection, Ohio.

Estimate: $2,000-$4,000

64135

FROM A PRIVATE COLLECTION IN NORTH TEXAS

MAURICE BRAUN (American, 1877-1941)
Landscape
Oil on artist's board
8 x 10 inches (20.3 x 25.4 cm)
Signed lower left: *Maurice Braun*

Estimate: $4,000-$6,000

64136

MARTIN LEWIS (American, 1881-1962)
Wet Saturday, 1920
Drypoint on paper
10 x 10-1/2 inches (25.4 x 26.7 cm)
Signed in margin lower right: *Martin Lewis imp-*

PROVENANCE:
Collection of Jane and Bert Gray, San Antonio, Texas.

EXHIBITED:
McNay Art Museum, San Antonio, Texas, "Close to Home: San Antonio Collects Works on Paper," January 16-March 17, 1996.

Estimate: $5,000-$7,000

64137

ALFREDO RAMOS MARTÍNEZ (Mexican, 1872-1946)
Still Life with Hydrangeas, 1917
Pastel on paper
36-3/4 x 28-1/2 inches (93.3 x 72.4 cm)
Signed and dated lower right: *Ramos Martinez / New York 1917*

Estimate: $4,000-$6,000

64138

PROPERTY FROM A PRIVATE COLLECTION, SAN DIEGO

GUY CARLETON WIGGINS (American, 1883-1962)
A Walk Along the Park, 1960
Oil on canvas
30 x 25 inches (76.2 x 63.5 cm)
Signed lower left: *Guy Wiggins*
Inscribed verso: *A Walk Along the Park/ Guy Wiggins/ 1960*

PROVENANCE:
Collection of Campbell H. Elkins, Lubbock, Texas;
Jerome H. Sharpe, San Diego, California, by bequest from the above.

A letter of authenticity from Guy Wiggins, Jr. accompanies this lot.

Estimate: $25,000-$35,000

THOMAS HART BENTON (American, 1889-1975)
Preliminary Study for "Romance", circa 1931
Gouache, tempera and graphite on gessoed board
12 x 11 inches (30.5 x 27.9 cm)

PROVENANCE:
The artist's daughter, Jessie Benton;
Private collection, Chicago, acquired from the above.

This work is a preliminary study for one of the most tender paintings of Thomas Hart Benton's career--Romance of 1931-32, in the Michener Collection, Blanton Museum of Art, University of Texas at Austin. The present owner acquired it directly from Thomas Hart Benton's daughter, Jessie, approximately 25 years ago.

Of the three known preliminary tempera studies for *Romance*, which feature an African-American couple strolling in the moonlight, the present panel is, in the opinion of Benton expert Dr. Henry Adams, most likely the earliest of the three. Several factors argue for its status as Benton's initial conception for *Romance*, a highly finished work in egg tempera with oil glazes on panel, which quickly became one of the artist's most celebrated easel paintings from the 1930s. In 1938, *Romance* was sent to Paris as part of an exhibition of American painting organized by the Museum of Modern Art.

Unlike the other two known preliminary studies for *Romance* documented in the Benton files of Owen Galleries, New York, which is preparing the Thomas Hart Benton catalogue raisonné, the present sketch is proportionally much squarer. The other two sketches are both taller and thinner, and thus are proportionally closer to the finished painting, which is longer and narrower, accentuating the monumentality of the couple. At some point early in his preparatory process, Benton clearly felt that the taller and narrower format helped accentuate the attenuated figures which were the compositional and emotional heart of his design.

Additionally, this study is considerably brushier and more rapidly painted than the other two known studies, factors which Dr. Adams regards as excellent indicators of the artist's initial idea. Benton was a fascinating artist in the way he developed a personal protocol for developing a visual idea from its initial inspiration, through compositional sketches in pencil, then black and white tonal studies in paint, then color studies, then sometimes detailed drawings of key parts of the design such as faces and still life motifs, until he undertook the final work of art itself on a large scale support. Since no pencil drawings for this work survive, and this panel is absolutely chock full of pencil lines, it seems that it probably doubled as Benton's initial drawing and initial painted tonal sketch in which he worked out the general relationships between the figures and landscape motifs. Indeed, upon close inspection, the rapidity by which Benton drew boldly on top of the paint--even scratching through the paint film itself to correct the poses, and refine the outlines--is fully evident. It is a marvelous example of Benton's willingness to sacrifice surface effects to 'get it right.' There's a toughness to his approach, which matches the clarity of his vision.

In addition to being a drawing plus a tonal study en grisaille, this fascinating panel also serves, in effect, as the first color study for the composition of *Romance*. Once the tonal relationships were worked out, Benton added color to this study, primarily various shades of blue in the sky, and the earthy browns describing most of the other features. One of the most curious and interesting passages is the intense blue-green patch of color between the branches of the tree which reads either as leaves or possibly just an enriched hue to experiment with the depth of the sky color. In some ways, this study is a more naturalistic portrayal of moonlight than the finished work: moonlight has a way of leeching color out of a scene. A comparison of this painted sketch with the final work in Austin shows Benton introducing a much broader range of color into the final design--in the bright red dress of the woman, delicate pink in her hat, and the golden glow of light on the ground. In reality, those colors would be much less legible in the moonlight.

According to Henry Adams: "Benton understood that romance is awkward, even a bit dorky. And it's also tender and magical. He wanted to capture that tension. Amazingly, for the 1930s, he chose to picture the concept of romance with an African-American couple.   Some people have accused Benton of being a racist, but I think he was actually just the opposite. He was asking white people to empathize with African-Americans, in fact, to identify with them.   While they don't fit white movie star stereotypes of what it is to be handsome, in some uncanny way these two people couldn't be more beautiful. They're perfectly in harmony with the dark silhouettes of the moss-covered trees and the romantic quality of the moonlit night. They're the embodiment of romance. Curiously, when I worked on a film on Benton with Ken Burns this was a painting that he kept mentioning and coming back to. For some reason he clearly identified with it. I think it was probably his favorite Benton painting."

We are grateful to Henry Adams for his scholarly generosity. We thank him for examining this painting through high resolution photographs, and endorsing a full attribution to Thomas Hart Benton on the basis of them.

Estimate: $25,000-$35,000

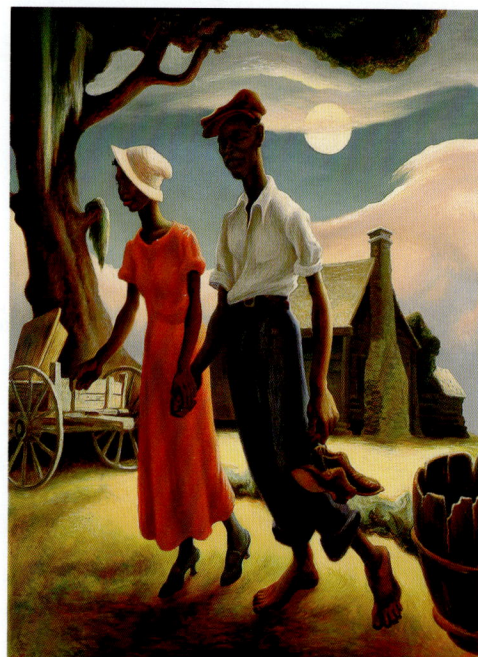

Blanton Museum of Art, the University of Texas at Austin, Gift of Mari and James A. Michener, 1991. Art © T. H. Benton and R. P. Benton Testamentary Trusts/UMB Bank Trustee/Licensed by VAGA, New York, NY

Photo: Rick Hall

64140

HUGHIE LEE-SMITH (American, 1915-1999)
Portrait of a Young Man (Said to be a Self-Portrait of the Artist), 1954
Oil on masonite
8 x 12 inches (20.3 x 30.5 cm)
Signed and dated upper left: *Lee-Smith / '54*

Estimate: $8,000-$12,000

64141

HUGHIE LEE-SMITH (American, 1915-1999)
Untitled (Landscape)
Watercolor on board
13-3/4 x 20-3/4 inches (34.9 x 52.7 cm)
Signed and dated lower right: *Lee.Smith / '53*

Estimate: $3,000-$5,000

64142

HUGHIE LEE-SMITH (American, 1915-1999)
The Hill, circa late 1950s early 1960s
Oil on canvas
24 x 32-1/4 inches (61.0 x 81.9 cm)
Signed lower right: *Lee-Smith*

Estimate: $25,000-$35,000

64143

ELIZABETH CATLETT (American, b. 1915)
Naima
Bronze with brown patina and polychrome
10 x 10 inches (25.4 x 25.4 cm)
Initialed on base: *EC*

Estimate: $10,000-$15,000

64144

LOIS MAILOU JONES (American, 1905-1998)
Floral Still Life, 1944
Watercolor on paper
19 x 13 inches (48.3 x 33.0 cm)
Signed and dated lower right: *Lois M / Jones '44*

Estimate: $2,000-$3,000

64145

HUGHIE LEE-SMITH (American, 1915-1999)

Rooftop and Landscape Study with Figure: A Double-Sided Work, circa 1952-1957

Oil on canvas

18 x 24 inches (45.7 x 61.0 cm)

Signed lower left: *Lee-Smith*

Estimate: $20,000-$30,000

64146

ROMARE HOWARD BEARDEN (American, 1914-1988)
Soldier at the Door, circa 1947-48
Watercolor on paper
23 x 17 inches (58.4 x 43.2 cm)
Signed lower right: *Bearden*

PROVENANCE:
Skinner, Inc., Boston, *American and European Paintings*, May 15, 2009, lot 382;
Acquired by the present owner from the above.

Estimate: $8,000-$10,000

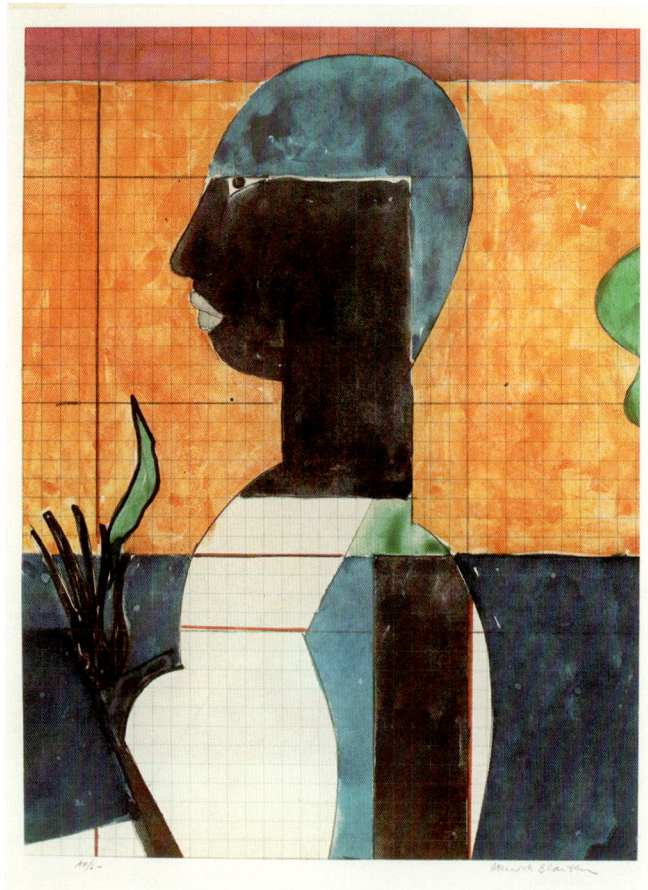

64147

ROMARE HOWARD BEARDEN (American, 1914-1988)
Here Begins Medicine, circa 1970
Offset lithograph
22 x 16-1/2 inches (55.9 x 41.9 cm)
Ed. AP/2
Signed in graphite lower right: *Romare Bearden*

Estimate: $2,000-$3,000

64148

JACOB LAWRENCE (American, 1917-2000)
Revolt on the Amistad, 1989
Color Screenprint
35 x 25-1/2 inches (88.9 x 64.8 cm)
Ed: 84/120
Signed and dated lower right margin: *Jacob Lawrence 1989*

This lot is accompanied by a letter of authenticity from Workshop, Inc., Washington, D.C. signed by the artist and dated "Thanksgiving 1989".

Estimate: $3,000-$5,000

64149

ROMARE HOWARD BEARDEN (American, 1914-1988)
Mother and Child from Conspiracy: The Artist as Witness, 1971
Color screenprint
24 x 18 inches (61.0 x 45.7 cm)
Ed. 36/150
Signed in graphite lower left edge: *romare bearden*

Estimate: $2,500-$3,500

64150

JACOB LAWRENCE (American, 1917-2000)
People in Other Rooms (Harlem Street Scene), 1975
Color screenprint
24-1/2 x 18-1/2 inches (62.2 x 47.0 cm)
Ed. 5/150
Signed and dated in graphite lower right: *Jacob Lawrence — 1975*
Titled in graphite lower center: *Harlem Street Scene*

Estimate: $4,000-$6,000

64151

ROWLAND HILDER (American/British, 1905-2005)
Ship in Full Sail, 1930
Charcoal, watercolor, and gouache on board
21 x 28-1/2 inches (53.3 x 72.4 cm)
Signed and dated lower right: *Rowland Hidler 1930*

Estimate: $1,500-$2,500

64152

EDMUND LEWANDOWSKI (American, 1914-1998)
Cabin Class, 1992
Gouache on paper
18-1/2 x 26-1/4 inches (47.0 x 66.7 cm)
Signed and dated lower right: *Edmund Lewandowski 1992*

PROVENANCE:
Keogh Riehlman Fine Art, New York (label verso).

Estimate: $2,500-$3,500

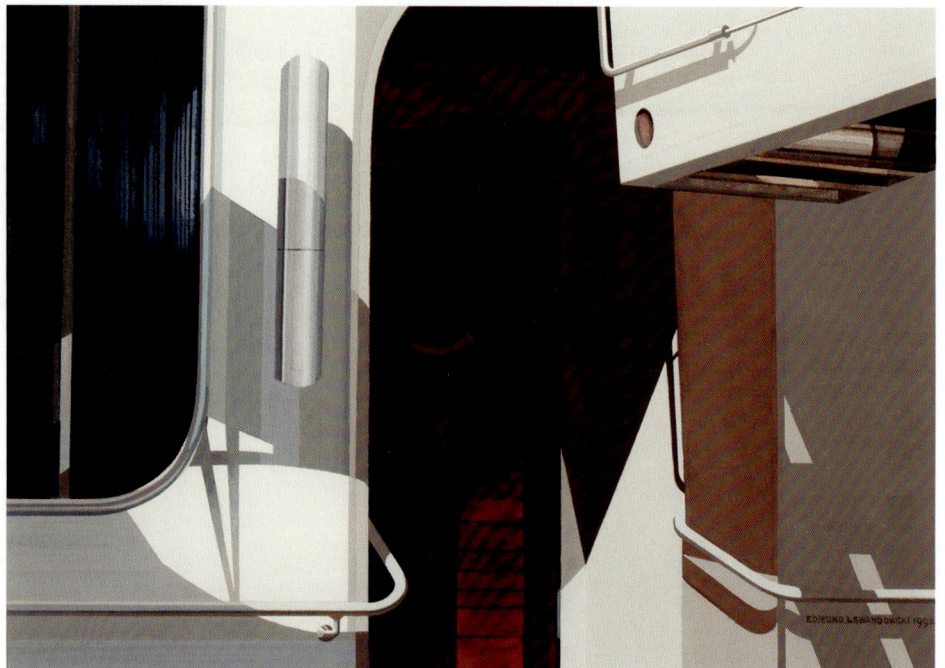

End of Auction

Terms and Conditions of Auction

Auctioneer and Auction:

1. This Auction is presented by Heritage Auction Galleries, a d/b/a/ of Heritage Auctions, Inc., or its affiliates Heritage Numismatic Auctions, Inc., or Heritage Vintage Sports Auctions, Inc., or Currency Auctions of America, Inc., as identified with the applicable licensing information on the title page of the catalog or on the HA.com Internet site (the "Auctioneer"). The Auction is conducted under these Terms and Conditions of Auction and applicable state and local law. Announcements and corrections from the podium and those made through the Terms and Conditions of Auctions appearing on the Internet at HA.com supersede those in the printed catalog.

Buyer's Premium:

2. On bids placed through Auctioneer, a Buyer's Premium of fifteen percent (15%) will be added to the successful hammer price bid on lots in Coin, Currency, and Firearms Auctions or nineteen and one-half percent (19.5%) on lots in all other Auctions. There is a minimum Buyer's Premium of $14.00 per lot. In Gallery Auctions (sealed bid auctions of mostly bulk numismatic material), the Buyer's Premium is 19.5%.

Auction Venues:

3. The following Auctions are conducted solely on the Internet: Heritage Weekly Internet Auctions (Coin, Currency, Comics, Rare Books, Jewelry & Watches, Guitars & Musical Instruments, and Vintage Movie Posters); Heritage Monthly Internet Auctions (Sports, World Coins and Rare Wine). Signature® Auctions and Grand Format Auctions accept bids from the Internet, telephone, fax, or mail first, followed by a floor bidding session; HeritageLive! and real- time telephone bidding are available to registered clients during these auctions.

Bidders:

4. Any person participating or registering for the Auction agrees to be bound by and accepts these Terms and Conditions of Auction ("Bidder(s)").
5. All Bidders must meet Auctioneer's qualifications to bid. Any Bidder who is not a client in good standing of the Auctioneer may be disqualified at Auctioneer's sole option and will not be awarded lots. Such determination may be made by Auctioneer in its sole and unlimited discretion, at any time prior to, during, or even after the close of the Auction. Auctioneer reserves the right to exclude any person from the auction.
6. If an entity places a bid, then the person executing the bid on behalf of the entity agrees to personally guarantee payment for any successful bid.

Credit:

7. Bidders who have not established credit with the Auctioneer must either furnish satisfactory credit information (including two collectibles-related business references) well in advance of the Auction or supply valid credit card information. Bids placed through our Interactive Internet program will only be accepted from pre-registered Bidders; Bidders who are not members of HA.com or affiliates should pre-register at least 48 hours before the start of the first session (exclusive of holidays or weekends) to allow adequate time to contact references. Credit may be granted at the discretion of Auctioneer. Additionally Bidders who have not previously established credit or who wish to bid in excess of their established credit history may be required to provide their social security number or the last four digits thereof to us so a credit check may be performed prior to Auctioneer's acceptance of a bid.

Bidding Options:

8. Bids in Signature® Auctions or Grand Format Auctions may be placed as set forth in the printed catalog section entitled "Choose your bidding method." For auctions held solely on the Internet, see the alternatives on HA.com. Review at HA.com/common/howtobid.php.
9. Presentment of Bids: Non-Internet bids (including but not limited to podium, fax, phone and mail bids) are treated similar to floor bids in that they must be on-increment or at a half increment (called a cut bid). Any podium, fax, phone, or mail bids that do not conform to a full or half increment will be rounded up or down to the nearest full or half increment and this revised amount will be considered your high bid.
10. Auctioneer's Execution of Certain Bids. Auctioneer cannot be responsible for your errors in bidding, so carefully check that every bid is entered correctly. When identical mail or FAX bids are submitted, preference is given to the first received. To ensure the greatest accuracy, your written bids should be entered on the standard printed bid sheet and be received at Auctioneer's place of business at least two business days before the Auction start. Auctioneer is not responsible for executing mail bids or FAX bids received on or after the day the first lot is sold, nor Internet bids submitted after the published closing time; nor is Auctioneer responsible for proper execution of bids submitted by telephone, mail, FAX, e-mail, Internet, or in person once the Auction begins. Bids placed electronically via the internet may not be withdrawn until your written request is received and acknowledged by Auctioneer (FAX: 214-443-8425); such requests must state the reason, and may constitute grounds for withdrawal of bidding privileges. Lots won by mail Bidders will not be delivered at the Auction unless prearranged.
11. Caveat as to Bid Increments. Bid increments (over the current bid level) determine the lowest amount you may bid on a particular lot. Bids greater than one increment over the current bid can be any whole dollar amount. It is possible under several circumstances for winning bids to be between increments, sometimes only $1 above the previous increment. Please see: "How can I lose by less than an increment?" on our website. Bids will be accepted in whole dollar amounts only. No "buy" or "unlimited" bids will be accepted.

The following chart governs current bidding increments.

Current Bid	Bid Increment	Current Bid	Bid Increment
<$10	$1	$20,000 - $29,999	$2,000
$10 - $29	$2	$30,000 - $49,999	$2,500
$30 - $49	$3	$50,000 - $99,999	$5,000
$50 - $99	$5	$100,000 - $199,999	$10,000
$100 - $199	$10	$200,000 - $299,999	$20,000
$200 - $299	$20	$300,000 - $499,999	$25,000
$300 - $499	$25	$500,000 - $999,999	$50,000
$500 - $999	$50	$1,000,000 - $1,999,999	$100,000
$1,000 - $1,999	$100	$2,000,000 - $2,999,999	$200,000
$2,000 - $2,999	$200	$3,000,000 - $4,999,999	$250,000
$3,000 - $4,999	$250	$5,000,000 - $9,999,999	$500,000
$5,000 - $9,999	$500	>$10,000,000	$1,000,000
$10,000 - $19,999	$1,000		

12. If Auctioneer calls for a full increment, a bidder may request Auctioneer to accept a bid at half of the increment ("Cut Bid") only once per lot. After offering a Cut Bid, bidders may continue to participate only at full increments. Off-increment bids may be accepted by the Auctioneer at Signature® Auctions and Grand Format Auctions. If the Auctioneer solicits bids other than the expected increment, these bids will not be considered Cut Bids.

Conducting the Auction:

13. Notice of the consignor's liberty to place bids on his lots in the Auction is hereby made in accordance with Article 2 of the Texas Business and Commercial Code. A "Minimum Bid" is an amount below which the lot will not sell. THE CONSIGNOR OF PROPERTY MAY PLACE WRITTEN "Minimum Bids" ON HIS LOTS IN ADVANCE OF THE AUCTION; ON SUCH LOTS, IF THE HAMMER PRICE DOES NOT MEET THE "Minimum Bid", THE CONSIGNOR MAY PAY A REDUCED COMMISSION ON THOSE LOTS. "Minimum Bids" are generally posted online several days prior to the Auction closing. For any successful bid placed by a consignor on his Property on the Auction floor, or by any means during the live session, or after the "Minimum Bid" for an Auction have been posted, we will require the consignor to pay full Buyer's Premium and Seller's Commissions on such lot.
14. The highest qualified Bidder recognized by the Auctioneer shall be the Buyer. In the event of a tie bid, the earliest bid received or recognized wins. In the event of any dispute between any Bidders at an Auction, Auctioneer may at his sole discretion reoffer the lot. Auctioneer's decision and declaration of the winning Bidder shall be final and binding upon all Bidders. Bids properly offered, whether by floor Bidder or other means of bidding, may on occasion be missed or go unrecognized; in such cases, the Auctioneer may declare the recognized bid accepted as the winning bid, regardless of whether a competing bid may have been higher.
15. Auctioneer reserves the right to refuse to honor any bid or to limit the amount of any bid, in its sole discretion. A bid is considered not made in "Good Faith" when made by an insolvent or irresponsible person, a person under the age of eighteen, or is not supported by satisfactory credit, collectibles references, or otherwise. Regardless of the disclosure of his identity, any bid by a consignor or his agent on a lot consigned by him is deemed to be made in "Good Faith." Any person apparently appearing on the OFAC list is not eligible to bid.
16. Nominal Bids. The Auctioneer in its sole discretion may reject nominal bids, small opening bids, or very nominal advances. If a lot bearing estimates fails to open for 40–60% of the low estimate, the Auctioneer may pass the item or may place a protective bid on behalf of the consignor.
17. Lots bearing bidding estimates shall open at Auctioneer's discretion (approximately 50%-60% of the low estimate). In the event that no bid meets or exceeds that opening amount, the lot shall pass as unsold.
18. All items are to be purchased per lot as numerically indicated and no lots will be broken. Auctioneer reserves the right to withdraw, prior to the close, any lots from the Auction.
19. Auctioneer reserves the right to rescind the sale in the event of nonpayment, breach of a warranty, disputed ownership, auctioneer's clerical error or omission in exercising bids and reserves, or for any other reason and in Auctioneer's sole discretion. In cases of nonpayment, Auctioneer's election to void a sale does not relieve the Bidder from their obligation to pay Auctioneer its fees (seller's and buyer's premium) and any other damages or expenses pertaining to the lot.
20. Auctioneer occasionally experiences Internet and/or Server service outages, and Auctioneer periodically schedules system downtime for maintenance and other purposes, during which Bidders cannot participate or place bids. If such outages occur, we may at our discretion extend bidding for the Auction. Bidders unable to place their Bids through the Internet are directed to contact Client Services at 1-800-872-6467.
21. The Auctioneer, its affiliates, or their employees consign items to be sold in the Auction, and may bid on those lots or any other lots. Auctioneer or affiliates expressly reserve the right to modify any such bids at any time prior to the hammer based upon data made known to the Auctioneer or its affiliates. The Auctioneer may extend advances, guarantees, or loans to certain consignors.
22. The Auctioneer has the right to sell certain unsold items after the close of the Auction. Such lots shall be considered sold during the Auction and all these Terms and Conditions shall apply to such sales including but not limited to the Buyer's Premium, return rights, and disclaimers.

Payment:

23. All sales are strictly for cash in United States dollars (including U.S. currency, bank wire, cashier checks, travelers checks, eChecks, and bank money orders, all subject to reporting requirements). All are subject to clearing and funds being received in Auctioneer's account before delivery of the purchases. Auctioneer reserves the right to determine if a check constitutes "good funds" when drawn on a U.S. bank for ten days, and thirty days when drawn on an international bank. Credit Card (Visa or Master Card only) and PayPal payments may be accepted up to $10,000 from non-dealers at the sole discretion of the Auctioneer, subject to the following limitations: a) sales are only to the cardholder, b) purchases are shipped to the cardholder's registered and verified address, c) Auctioneer may pre-approve the cardholder's credit line, d) a credit card transaction may not be used in conjunction with any other financing or extended terms offered by the Auctioneer, and must transact immediately upon invoice presentation, e) rights of return are governed by these Terms and Conditions, which supersede those conditions promulgated by the card issuer, f) floor Bidders must present their card.
24. Payment is due upon closing of the Auction session, or upon presentment of an invoice. Auctioneer reserves the right to void an invoice if payment in full is not received within 7 days after the close of the Auction. In cases of nonpayment, Auctioneer's election to void a sale does not relieve the Bidder from their obligation to pay Auctioneer its fees (seller's and buyer's premium) on the lot and any other damages pertaining to the lot.
25. Lots delivered to you, or your representative in the States of Texas, California, New York, or other states where the Auction may be held, are subject to all applicable state and local taxes, unless appropriate permits are on file with Auctioneer. (Note: Coins are only subject to sales tax in California on invoices under $1500 and in Texas on invoices under $1000. Check the Web site at: http://coins.ha.com/c/ref/sales-tax.zx for more details.) Bidder agrees to pay Auctioneer the actual amount of tax due in the event that sales tax is not properly collected due to: 1) an expired, inaccurate, inappropriate tax certificate or declaration, 2) an incorrect interpretation of the applicable statute, 3) or any other reason. The appropriate form or certificate must be on file at and verified by Auctioneer five days prior to Auction or tax must be paid; only if such form or certificate is received by Auctioneer within 4 days after the Auction can a refund of tax paid be made. Lots from different Auctions may not be aggregated for sales tax purposes.
26. In the event that a Bidder's payment is dishonored upon presentment(s), Bidder shall pay the maximum statutory processing fee set by applicable state law. If you attempt to pay via eCheck and your financial institution denies this transfer from your bank account, or the payment cannot be completed using the selected funding source, you agree to complete payment using your credit card on file.
27. If any Auction invoice submitted by Auctioneer is not paid in full when due, the unpaid balance will bear interest at the highest rate permitted by law from the date of invoice until paid. Any invoice not paid when due will bear a three percent (3%) late fee on the invoice amount or three percent (3%) of any installment that is past due. If the Auctioneer refers any invoice to an attorney for collection, the buyer agrees to pay attorney's fees, court costs, and other collection costs incurred by Auctioneer. If Auctioneer assigns collection to its in-house legal staff, such attorney's time expended on the matter shall be compensated at a rate comparable to the hourly rate of independent attorneys.
28. In the event a successful Bidder fails to pay any amounts due, Auctioneer reserves the right to sell the lot(s) securing the invoice to any underbidders in the Auction that the lot(s) appeared, or at subsequent private or public sale, or relist the lot(s) in a future auction conducted by Auctioneer. A defaulting Bidder agrees to pay for the reasonable costs of resale (including a 10% seller's commission, if consigned to an auction conducted by Auctioneer). The defaulting Bidder is liable to pay any difference between his total original invoice for the lot(s), plus any applicable interest, and the net proceeds for the lot(s) if sold at private sale or the subsequent hammer price of the lot(s) less the 10% seller's commissions, if sold at an Auctioneer's auction.
29. Auctioneer reserves the right to require payment in full in good funds before delivery of the merchandise.

Terms and Conditions of Auction

30. Auctioneer shall have a lien against the merchandise purchased by the buyer to secure payment of the Auction invoice. Auctioneer is further granted a lien and the right to retain possession of any other property of the buyer then held by the Auctioneer or its affiliates to secure payment of any Auction invoice or any other amounts due the Auctioneer or affiliates from the buyer. With respect to these lien rights, Auctioneer shall have all the rights of a secured creditor under Article 9 of the Texas Uniform Commercial Code, including but not limited to the right of sale. In addition, with respect to payment of the Auction invoice(s), the buyer waives any and all rights of offset he might otherwise have against the Auctioneer and the consignor of the merchandise included on the invoice. If a Bidder owes Auctioneer or its affiliates on any account, Auctioneer and its affiliates shall have the right to offset such unpaid account by any credit balance due Bidder, and it may secure by possessory lien any unpaid amount by any of the Bidder's property in their possession.
31. Title shall not pass to the successful Bidder until all invoices are paid in full. It is the responsibility of the buyer to provide adequate insurance coverage for the items once they have been delivered to a common carrier or third-party shipper.

Delivery; Shipping; and Handling Charges:

32. Buyer is liable for shipping and handling. Please refer to Auctioneer's website www.HA.com/common/shipping.php for the latest charges or call Auctioneer. Auctioneer is unable to combine purchases from other auctions or affiliates into one package for shipping purposes. Lots won will be shipped in a commercially reasonable time after payment in good funds for the merchandise and the shipping fees is received or credit extended, except when third-party shipment occurs.
33. Successful international Bidders shall provide written shipping instructions, including specified customs declarations, to the Auctioneer for any lots to be delivered outside of the United States. NOTE: Declaration value shall be the item'(s) hammer price together with its buyer's premium and Auctioneer shall use the correct harmonized code for the lot. Domestic Buyers on lots designated for third-party shipment must designate the common carrier, accept risk of loss, and prepay shipping costs.
34. All shipping charges will be borne by the successful Bidder. On all domestic shipments, any risk of loss during shipment will be borne by Heritage until the shipping carrier's confirmation of delivery to the address of record in Auctioneer's file (carrier's confirmation is conclusive to prove delivery to Bidder; if the client has a Signature release on file with the carrier, the package is considered delivered without Signature) or delivery by Heritage to Bidder's selected third-party shipper. On all foreign shipments, any risk of loss during shipment will be borne by the Bidder following Auctioneer's delivery to the Bidder's designated common carrier or third-party shipper.
35. Due to the nature of some items sold, it shall be the responsibility for the successful Bidder to arrange pick-up and shipping through third-parties; as to such items Auctioneer shall have no liability. Failure to pick-up or arrange shipping in a timely fashion (within ten days) shall subject Lots to storage and moving charges, including a $100 administration fee plus $10 daily storage for larger items and $5.00 daily for smaller items (storage fee per item) after 35 days. In the event the Lot is not removed within ninety days, the Lot may be offered for sale to recover any past due storage or moving fees, including a 10% Seller's Commission.
36. The laws of various countries regulate the import or export of certain plant and animal properties, including (but not limited to) items made of (or including) ivory, whalebone, turtleshell, coral, crocodile, or other wildlife. Transport of such lots may require special licenses for export, import, or both. Bidder is responsible for: 1) obtaining all information on such restricted items for both export and import; 2) obtaining all such licenses and/or permits. Delay or failure to obtain any such license or permit does not relieve the buyer of timely compliance with standard payment terms. For further information, please contact Ron Brackemyre at 800-872-6467 ext. 1312.
37. Any request for shipping verification for undelivered packages must be made within 30 days of shipment by Auctioneer.

Cataloging, Warranties and Disclaimers:

38. NO WARRANTY, WHETHER EXPRESSED OR IMPLIED, IS MADE WITH RESPECT TO ANY DESCRIPTION CONTAINED IN THIS AUCTION OR ANY SECOND OPINE. Any description of the items or second opine contained in this Auction is for the sole purpose of identifying the items for those Bidders who do not have the opportunity to view the lots prior to bidding, and no description of items has been made part of the basis of the bargain or has created any express warranty that the goods would conform to any description made by Auctioneer. Color variations can be expected in any electronic or printed imaging, and are not grounds for the return of any lot. NOTE: Auctioneer, in specified auction venues, for example, Fine Art, may have express written warranties and you are referred to those specific terms and conditions. .
39. Auctioneer is selling only such right or title to the items being sold as Auctioneer may have by virtue of consignment agreements on the date of auction and disclaims any warranty of title to the Property. Auctioneer disclaims any warranty of merchantability or fitness for any particular purposes. All images, descriptions, sales data, and archival records are the exclusive property of Auctioneer, and may be used by Auctioneer for advertising, promotion, archival records, and any other uses deemed appropriate.
40. Translations of foreign language documents may be provided as a convenience to interested parties. Auctioneer makes no representation as to the accuracy of those translations and will not be held responsible for errors in bidding arising from inaccuracies in translation.
41. Auctioneer disclaims all liability for damages, consequential or otherwise, arising out of or in connection with the sale of any Property by Auctioneer to Bidder. No third party may rely on any benefit of these Terms and Conditions and any rights, if any, established hereunder are personal to the Bidder and may not be assigned. Any statement made by the Auctioneer is an opinion and does not constitute a warranty or representation. No employee of Auctioneer may alter these Terms and Conditions, and, unless signed by a principal of Auctioneer, any such alteration is null and void.
42. Auctioneer shall not be liable for breakage of glass or damage to frames (patent or latent); such defects, in any event, shall not be a basis for any claim for return or reduction in purchase price.

Release:

43. In consideration of participation in the Auction and the placing of a bid, Bidder expressly releases Auctioneer, its officers, directors and employees, its affiliates, and its outside experts that provide second opines, from any and all claims, cause of action, chose of action, whether at law or equity or any arbitration or mediation rights existing under the rules of any professional society or affiliation based upon the assigned description, or a derivative theory, breach of warranty express or implied, representation or other matter set forth within these Terms and Conditions of Auction or otherwise. In the event of a claim, Bidder agrees that such rights and privileges conferred therein are strictly construed as specifically declared herein; e.g., authenticity, typographical error, etc. and are the exclusive remedy. Bidder, by non-compliance to these express terms of a granted remedy, shall waive any claim against Auctioneer.
44. Notice: Some Property sold by Auctioneer are inherently dangerous e.g. firearms, cannons, and small items that may be swallowed or ingested or may have latent defects all of which may cause harm to a person. Purchaser accepts all risk of loss or damage from its purchase of these items and Auctioneer disclaims any liability whether under contract or tort for damages and losses, direct or inconsequential, and expressly disclaims any warranty as to safety or usage of any lot sold.

Dispute Resolution and Arbitration Provision:

45. By placing a bid or otherwise participating in the auction, Bidder accepts these Terms and Conditions of Auction, and specifically agrees to the dispute resolution provided herein. Consumer disputes shall be resolved through court litigation which has an exclusive Dallas, Texas venue clause and jury waiver. Non-consumer dispute shall be determined in binding arbitration which arbitration replaces the right to go to court, including the right to a jury trial.
46. Auctioneer in no event shall be responsible for consequential damages, incidental damages, compensatory damages, or any other damages arising or claimed to be arising from the auction of any lot. In the event that Auctioneer cannot deliver the lot or subsequently it is established that the lot lacks title, or other transfer or condition issue is claimed, in such cases the sole remedy shall be limited to rescission of sale and refund of the amount paid by Bidder; in no case shall Auctioneer's maximum liability exceed the high bid on that lot, which bid shall be deemed for all purposes the value of the lot. After one year has elapsed, Auctioneer's maximum liability shall be limited to any commissions and fees Auctioneer earned on that lot.
47. In the event of an attribution error, Auctioneer may at its sole discretion, correct the error on the Internet, or, if discovered at a later date, to refund the buyer's purchase price without further obligation.
48. Dispute Resolution for Consumers and Non-Consumers: Any claim, dispute, or controversy in connection with, relating to and /or arising out of the Auction, participation in the Auction, award of lots, damages of claims to lots, descriptions, condition reports, provenance, estimates, return and warranty rights, any interpretation of these Terms and Conditions, any alleged verbal modification of these Terms and Conditions and/or any purported settlement whether asserted in contract, tort, under Federal or State statute or regulation shall or any other matter: a) if presented by a consumer, be exclusively heard by, and the parties consent to, exclusive in personam jurisdiction in the State District Courts of Dallas County, Texas. THE PARTIES EXPRESSLY WAIVE ANY RIGHT TO TRIAL BY JURY. Any appeals shall be solely pursued in the appellate courts of the State of Texas; or b) for any claimant other than a consumer, the claim shall be presented in confidential binding arbitration before a single arbitrator, that the parties may agree upon, selected from the JAMS list of Texas arbitrators. The case is not to be administrated by JAMS; however, if the parties cannot agree on an arbitrator, then JAMS shall appoint the arbitrator and it shall be conducted under JAMS rules. The locale shall be Dallas Texas. The arbitrator's award may be enforced in any court of competent jurisdiction. Any party on any claim involving the purchase or sale of numismatic or related items may elect arbitration through binding PNG arbitration. Any claim must be brought within one (1) year of the alleged breach, default or misrepresentation or the claim is waived. This agreement and any claims shall be determined and construed under Texas law. The prevailing party (party that is awarded substantial and material relief on its claim or defense) may be awarded its reasonable attorneys' fees and costs.
49. No claims of any kind can be considered after the settlements have been made with the consignors. Any dispute after the settlement date is strictly between the Bidder and consignor without involvement or responsibility of the Auctioneer.
50. In consideration of their participation in or application for the Auction, a person or entity (whether the successful Bidder, a Bidder, a purchaser and/or other Auction participant or registrant) agrees that all disputes in any way relating to, arising under, connected with, or incidental to these Terms and Conditions and purchases, or default in payment thereof, shall be arbitrated pursuant to the arbitration provision. In the event that any matter including actions to compel arbitration, construe the agreement, actions in aid or arbitration or otherwise needs to be litigated, such litigation shall be exclusively in the Courts of the State of Texas, in Dallas County, Texas, and if necessary the corresponding appellate courts. For such actions, the successful Bidder, purchaser, or Auction participant also expressly submits himself to the personal jurisdiction of the State of Texas.
51. These Terms & Conditions provide specific remedies for occurrences in the auction and delivery process. Where such remedies are afforded, they shall be interpreted strictly. Bidder agrees that any claim shall utilize such remedies; Bidder making a claim in excess of those remedies provided in these Terms and Conditions agrees that in no case whatsoever shall Auctioneer's maximum liability exceed the high bid on that lot, which bid shall be deemed for all purposes the value of the lot.

Miscellaneous:

52. Agreements between Bidders and consignors to effectuate a non-sale of an item at Auction, inhibit bidding on a consigned item to enter into a private sale agreement for said item, or to utilize the Auctioneer's Auction to obtain sales for non-selling consigned items subsequent to the Auction, are strictly prohibited. If a subsequent sale of a previously consigned item occurs in violation of this provision, Auctioneer reserves the right to charge Bidder the applicable Buyer's Premium and consignor a Seller's Commission as determined for each auction venue and by the terms of the seller's agreement.
53. Acceptance of these Terms and Conditions qualifies Bidder as a client who has consented to be contacted by Heritage in the future. In conformity with "do-not-call" regulations promulgated by the Federal or State regulatory agencies, participation by the Bidder is affirmative consent to being contacted at the phone number shown in his application and this consent shall remain in effect until it is revoked in writing. Heritage may from time to time contact Bidder concerning sale, purchase, and auction opportunities available through Heritage and its affiliates and subsidiaries.
54. Rules of Construction: Auctioneer presents properties in a number of collectible fields, and as such, specific venues have promulgated supplemental Terms and Conditions. Nothing herein shall be construed to waive the general Terms and Conditions of Auction by these additional rules and shall be construed to give force and effect to the rules in their entirety.

State Notices:

Notice as to an Auction in California. Auctioneer has in compliance with Title 2.95 of the California Civil Code as amended October 11, 1993 Sec. 1812.600, posted with the California Secretary of State its bonds for it and its employees, and the auction is being conducted in compliance with Sec. 2338 of the Commercial Code and Sec. 535 of the Penal Code.

Notice as to an Auction in New York City. These Terms and Conditions of Sale are designed to conform to the applicable sections of the New York City Department of Consumer Affairs Rules and Regulations as Amended. This sale is a Public Auction Sale conducted by Heritage Auction Galleries, Inc. #41513036. The New York City licensed auctioneers are: Sam Foose, #095260; Kathleen Guzman, #0762165; Nicholas Dawes, #1304724; Ed Beardsley, #1183220; Scott Peterson, #1306933; Andrea Voss, #1320558, who will conduct the Sale on behalf of Heritage Numismatic Auctions, Inc. (for Coins and Currency) and Heritage Auction Galleries Inc. (for other items). All lots are subject to: the consignor's rights to bid thereon in accord with these Terms and Conditions of Sale, consignor's option to receive advances on their consignments, and Auctioneer, in its sole discretion, may offer limited extended financing to registered bidders, in accord with Auctioneer's internal credit standards. A registered bidder may inquire whether a lot is subject to an advance or a reserve. Auctioneer has made advances to various consignors in this sale. On lots bearing an estimate, the term refers to a value range placed on an item by the Auctioneer in its sole opinion but the final price is determined by the bidders.

Notice as to an Auction in Texas. In compliance with TDLR rule 67.100(c)(1), notice is hereby provided that this auction is covered by a Recovery Fund administered by the Texas Department of Licensing and Regulation, P.O. Box 12157, Austin, Texas 78711 (512) 463-6599. Any complaints may be directed to the same address.

Notice as to an Auction in Ohio: Auction firm and Auctioneer are licensed by the Dept. of Agriculture, and either the licensee is bonded in favor of the state or an aggrieved person may initiate a claim against the auction recovery fund created in Section 4707.25 of the Revised Code as a result of the licensee's actions, whichever is applicable.

Rev. 7-25-11

Terms and Conditions of Auction

Additional Terms & Conditions:
FINE & DECORATIVE ARTS AUCTIONS

FINE AND DECORATIVE ARTS TERM A: LIMITED WARRANTY: Auctioneer warrants authorship, period or culture of each lot sold in this catalog as set out in the **BOLD**-face type heading in the catalog description of the lot, with the following exclusions. This warranty does not apply to:
i. authorship of any paintings, drawings or sculpture created prior to 1870, unless the lot is determined to be a counterfeit which has a value at the date of the claim for rescission which is materially less than the purchase price paid for the lot; or
ii. any catalog description where it was specifically mentioned that there is a conflict of specialist opinion on the authorship of a lot; or
iii. authorship which on the date of sale was in accordance with the then generally accepted opinion of scholars and specialists, despite the subsequent discovery of new information, whether historical or physical, concerning the artist or craftsman, his students, school, workshop or followers; or
iv. the identification of periods or dates of execution which may be proven inaccurate by means of scientific processes not generally accepted for use until after publication of the catalog, or which were unreasonably expensive or impractical to use at the time of publication of the catalog. The term counterfeit is defined as a modern fake or forgery, made less than fifty years ago with the intent to deceive. The authenticity of signatures, monograms, initials or other similar indications of authorship is expressly excluded as a controlling factor in determining whether a work is a counterfeit under the meaning of these Terms and Conditions of Auction.

FINE AND DECORATIVE ARTS TERM B: GLOSSARY OF TERMS: Terms used in this catalog have the following meanings. Please note that all statements in this catalog, excluding those in **BOLD**-face type, regarding authorship, attribution, origin, date, age, provenance and condition are statements of opinion and are not treated as a statement of fact.
1. THOMAS MORAN
In our opinion, the work is by the artist.
2. ATTRIBUTED TO THOMAS MORAN
In our opinion, the work is of the period of the artist which may be whole or in part the work of the artist.
3. STUDIO, (CIRCLE OR WORKSHOP) OF THOMAS MORAN
In our opinion, the work is of the period and closely relates to his style.
4. SCHOOL OF THOMAS MORAN
In our opinion, the work is by a pupil or a follower of the artist.
5. MANNER OF THOMAS MORAN
In our opinion, the work is in the style of the artist and is of a later period.
6. AFTER THOMAS MORAN
In our opinion, this work is a copy of the artist.
7. ASCRIBED TO THOMAS MORAN
In our opinion, this work is not by the artist, however, previous scholarship has noted this to be a work by the artist.
8. SIGNED (OR DATED)
The work has a signature (or date) which is in our opinion is genuine.
9. BEARS SIGNATURE (OR DATE)
The work has a signature (or date) which in our opinion is not authentic.

FINE AND DECORATIVE ARTS TERM C: PRESENTMENT: The warranty as to authorship is provided for a period of one (1) year from the date of the auction and is only for the benefit of the original purchaser of record and is not transferable.

FINE AND DECORATIVE ARTS TERM D: The Auction is not on approval. Under extremely limited circumstances (e.g. gross cataloging error), not including attributions in **BOLD**-face type, which are addressed in Term F below, a purchaser who did not bid from the floor may request Auctioneer to evaluate voiding a sale; such request must be made in writing detailing the alleged gross error, and submission of the lot to Auctioneer must be pre-approved by Auctioneer. A bidder must notify the appropriate department head (check the inside front cover of the catalog or our website for a listing of department heads) in writing of the purchaser's request within three (3) days of the non-floor bidder's receipt of the lot. Any lot that is to be evaluated for return must be received in our offices within 40 days after Auction. AFTER THAT 40-DAY PERIOD, NO LOT MAY BE RETURNED FOR ANY REASON. Lots returned must be in the same condition as when sold and must include any Certificate of Authenticity. No lots purchased by floor bidders (including those bidders acting as agents for others) may be returned. Late remittance for purchases may be considered just cause to revoke all return privileges.

FINE AND DECORATIVE ARTS TERM E: The catalog descriptions are provided for identification purposes only. Bidders who intend to challenge a **BOLD**-face provision in the description of a lot must notify Auctioneer in writing within forty (40) days of the Auction's conclusion. In the event Auctioneer cannot deliver the lot or subsequently it is established that the lot lacks title or the **BOLD**-face section of description is incorrect, or other transfer or condition issue is claimed, Auctioneer's liability shall be limited to rescission of sale and refund of purchase price. In no case shall Auctioneer's maximum liability exceed the successful bid on that lot, which bid shall be deemed for all purposes the value of the lot. After one year has elapsed from the close of the Auction, Auctioneer's maximum liability shall be limited to any commissions and fees Auctioneer earned on that lot.

FINE AND DECORATIVE ARTS TERM F: Any claim as to authorship, provenance, authenticity, or other matter under the remedies provided in the Fine Arts Terms and Conditions or otherwise must be first transmitted to Auctioneer by credible and definitive evidence within the applicable claim period. Auctioneer, in processing the written claim, may require the Purchaser to obtain the written opinion of two recognized experts in the field who are mutually accepted by Auctioneer and Purchaser. Upon receipt of the two opinions, Auctioneer shall determine whether to rescind the sale. The Purchaser's claim must be presented in accord with the remedies provided herein and is subject to the limitations and restrictions provided (including within the described time limitations). Regardless of Purchaser's submissions there is no assurance after such presentment that Auctioneer will validate the claim. Authentication is not an exact science and contrary opinions may not be recognized by Auctioneer. Even if Auctioneer agrees with the contrary opinion of such authentication and provides a remedy within these Terms and Conditions or otherwise, our liability for reimbursement for bidder's third party opines shall not exceed $500. The right of rescission, return, or any other remedy provided in these Terms and Conditions, or any other applicable law, does not extend to authorship of any lot which at the date of Auction was in accordance with the then generally accepted opinion of scholars and specialists, despite the subsequent discovery of new information, whether historical or physical, concerning the artist, his students, school, workshop or followers. Purchaser by placing a bid expressly waives any claim or damage based on such subsequent information as described herein. It is specifically understood that any refund agreed to by the Auctioneer would be limited to the purchase price.

FINE AND DECORATIVE ARTS TERM G: Provenance and authenticity, excluding attributions in **BOLD**-face type, are guaranteed by neither the consignor nor Auctioneer. While every effort is made to determine provenance and authenticity, it is the responsibility of the Bidder to arrive at their own conclusion prior to bidding.

FINE AND DECORATIVE ARTS TERM H: On the fall of Auctioneer's hammer, Buyers of Fine Arts and Decorative Arts lots assumes full risk and responsibility for lot, including shipment by common carrier or third-party shipper, and must provide their own insurance coverage for shipments.

FINE AND DECORATIVE ARTS TERM I: Auctioneer complies with all Federal and State rules and regulations relating to the purchasing, registration and shipping of firearms. A purchaser is required to provide appropriate documents and the payment of associated fees, if any. Purchaser is responsible for providing a shipping address that is suitable for the receipt of a firearm.

Heritage Auction Galleries strongly encourages in-person inspection of lots by the Bidder. While Heritage is not obligated to provide a condition report of each lot, Bidders may feel free to contact the department for a Condition Report and Heritage will attempt to furnish one, but shall not be liable for failing to do so. Condition is often detailed online, but is not included in our catalogues. The Bidder should review online descriptions as the descriptions supercede catalog descriptions and those condition reports otherwise provided. Statements by Heritage regarding the condition of objects are for guidance only and should not be relied upon as statements of fact, and do not constitute a representation, warranty, or assumption of liability by Heritage. All lots offered regardless of a condition report are sold "AS IS".

For wiring instructions call the Credit department at 1-800-872-6467 or e-mail: CreditDept@HA.com

New York State Auctions Only

These Terms and Conditions of Sale are designed to conform to the applicable sections of the New York City Department of Consumer Affairs Rules and Regulations as Amended. This sale is a Public Auction Sale conducted by Heritage Auction Galleries, Inc. #41513036. The New York City licensed auctioneers are: Sam Foose, #095260; Kathleen Guzman, #0762165; Nicholas Dawes, #1304724; Ed Beardsley, #1183220; Scott Peterson, #1306933; Andrea Voss, #1320558, who will conduct the Sale on behalf of Heritage Numismatic Auctions, Inc. (for Coins and Currency) and Heritage Auction Galleries Inc. (for other items). All lots are subject to: the consignor's rights to bid thereon in accord with these Terms and Conditions of Auction, consignor's option to receive advances on their consignments, and Auctioneer, in its sole discretion, may offer limited extended financing to registered bidders, in accord with Auctioneer's internal credit standards. A registered bidder may inquire whether a lot is subject to an advance or a reserve. Auctioneer has made advances to various consignors in this sale. On lots bearing an estimate, the term refers to a value range placed on an item by the Auctioneer in its sole opinion but the final price is determined by the bidders.

Rev.12-23-10

How to Ship Your Purchases

Agent Shipping Release
Authorization form

Heritage Auction Galleries requires "Third Party Shipping" for certain items in this auction not picked up in person by the buyer. It shall be the responsibility of the successful bidder to arrange pick up and shipping through a third party; as to such items auctioneer shall have no liability.

Steps to follow:

1. Select a shipping company from the list below or a company of your choosing.

2. Complete, sign, and return an Agent Shipping Release Authorization form to Heritage (this form will automatically be emailed to you along with your winning bid(s) notice or may be obtained by calling Client Services at 866-835-3243). The completed form may be faxed to 214-409-1425.

3. Heritage Auctions' shipping department will coordinate with the shipping company you have selected to pick up your purchases.

Shippers that Heritage has used are listed below. However, you are not obligated to choose from the following and may provide Heritage with information of your preferred shipper.

Navis Pack & Ship	The Packing & Moving Center	Craters & Freighters
161 Pittsburgh St	2040 E. Arkansas Lane, Ste #222	2220 Merritt Drive, Suite 200
Dallas, TX 75207	Arlington, TX 76011	Garland, TX 75041
Ph: 972-870-1212	Ph: 817-795-1999	Ph: 972-840-8147
Fax: 214-409-9001	Fax: 214-409-9000	Fax: 214-780-5674
Navis.Dallas@GoNavis.com	thepackman@sbcglobal.net	dallas@cratersandfreighters.com

- It is the Third Party Shipper's responsibility to pack (or crate) and ship (or freight) your purchase to you. Please make all payment arrangements for shipping with your Shipper of choice.

- Any questions concerning Third Party Shipping can be addressed through our Client Services Department at 1-866-835-3243.

- Successful bidders are advised that pick-up or shipping arrangements should be made within ten (10) days of the auction or they may be subject to storage fees as stated in Heritage's Terms & Conditions of Auction, item 35.

VINTAGE & CONTEMPORARY
PHOTOGRAPHY AUCTION

NOVEMBER 19, 2011 | NEW YORK | LIVE & ONLINE

O. WINSTON LINK | *Hot Shot Eastbound at the Laeger Drive-In, West Virginia, 1956* | Gelatin silver, 1989 | Image: 15-1/2 x 19-1/4 in. | Estimate: $6,000 - $8,000
HA.com/5077-21014

Visit HA.com/5077 | Inquiries: 800-872-6467
ED JASTER | ext. 1288 | EdJ@HA.com | **RACHEL PEART** | ext. 1625 | RPeart@HA.com

For a free auction catalog in any category, plus a copy of *The Collector's Handbook* (combined value $65), visit HA.com/CATA25539 or call 866-835-3243 and reference code CATA25539.

Artist Index

Department Specialists

For the extensions below, please dial 800.872.6467

Comics & Comic Art
HA.com/Comics

Ed Jaster, Ext. 1288 • EdJ@HA.com

Lon Allen, Ext. 1261 • LonA@HA.com

Barry Sandoval, Ext. 1377 • BarryS@HA.com

Todd Hignite, Ext. 1790 • ToddH@HA.com

Fine Art

American, Western & European Art
HA.com/FineArt

Ed Jaster, Ext. 1288 • EdJ@HA.com

Marianne Berardi, Ph.D., Ext. 1506 • MarianneB@HA.com

Ariana Hartsock, Ext. 1283 • ArianaH@HA.com

Kirsty Buchanan, Ext. 1741 • KirstyB@HA.com

Deborah Solon, Ext. 1843 • DeborahS@HA.com

California Art
HA.com/FineArt

Alissa Ford, Ext. 1926 • AlissaF@HA.com

Deborah Solon, Ext. 1843 • DeborahS@HA.com

Decorative Arts & Design
HA.com/Decorative

Tim Rigdon, Ext. 1119 • TimR@HA.com

Karen Rigdon, Ext. 1723 • KarenR@HA.com

Nicholas Dawes, Ext. 1605 • NickD@HA.com

Carolyn Mani, Ext. 1677 • CarolynM@HA.com

Illustration Art
HA.com/Illustration

Ed Jaster, Ext. 1288 • EdJ@HA.com

Todd Hignite, Ext. 1790 • ToddH@HA.com

Lalique & Art Glass
HA.com/Design

Nicholas Dawes, Ext. 1605 • NickD@HA.com

Modern & Contemporary Art
HA.com/Modern

Frank Hettig, Ext. 1157 • FrankH@HA.com

Silver & Vertu
HA.com/Silver

Tim Rigdon, Ext. 1119 • TimR@HA.com

Karen Rigdon, Ext. 1723 • KarenR@HA.com

Texas Art
HA.com/TexasArt

Atlee Phillips, Ext. 1786 • AtleeP@HA.com

Vintage & Contemporary Photography
HA.com/ArtPhotography

Ed Jaster, Ext. 1288 • EdJ@HA.com

Rachel Peart, Ext. 1625 • RPeart@HA.com

Handbags & Luxury Accessories
HA.com/Luxury

Matt Rubinger, Ext. 1419 • MRubinger@HA.com

Historical

American Indian Art
HA.com/AmericanIndian

Delia Sullivan, Ext. 1343 • DeliaS@HA.com

Americana & Political
HA.com/Historical

Tom Slater, Ext. 1441 • TomS@HA.com

John Hickey, Ext. 1264 • JohnH@HA.com

Michael Riley, Ext. 1467 • MichaelR@HA.com

Don Ackerman, Ext. 1736 • DonA@HA.com

Arms & Armor
HA.com/Arms

Greg Martin, Ext. 1883 • GregM@HA.com

Jemison Beshears, Ext. 1886 • JemisonB@HA.com

Cliff Chappell, Ext. 1887 • CliffordC@HA.com

Roger Lake, Ext. 1884 • RogerL@HA.com

David Carde, Ext. 1881 • DavidC@HA.com

Civil War & Militaria
HA.com/CivilWar

Dennis Lowe, Ext. 1182 • DennisL@HA.com

Historical Manuscripts
HA.com/Manuscripts

Sandra Palomino, Ext. 1107 • SandraP@HA.com

Rare Books
HA.com/Books

James Gannon, Ext. 1609 • JamesG@HA.com

Joe Fay, Ext. 1544 • JoeF@HA.com

Space Exploration
HA.com/Space

John Hickey, Ext. 1264 • JohnH@HA.com

Michael Riley, Ext. 1467 • MichaelR@HA.com

Texana
HA.com/Historical

Sandra Palomino, Ext. 1107 • SandraP@HA.com

Jewelry
HA.com/Jewelry

Jill Burgum, Ext. 1697 • JillB@HA.com

Peggy Gottlieb, Ext. 1847 • PGottlieb@HA.com

Movie Posters
HA.com/MoviePosters

Grey Smith, Ext. 1367 • GreySm@HA.com

Bruce Carteron, Ext. 1551 • BruceC@HA.com

Music & Entertainment Memorabilia
HA.com/Entertainment

Margaret Barrett, Ext. 1912 • MargaretB@HA.com
Kristen Painter, Ext. 1149 • KristenP@HA.com
John Hickey, Ext. 1264 • JohnH@HA.com
Garry Shrum, Ext. 1585 • GarryS@HA.com

Vintage Guitars & Musical Instruments
HA.com/Guitar

Mike Gutierrez, Ext. 1183 • MikeG@HA.com
Isaiah Evans, Ext. 1201 • IsaiahE@HA.com

Natural History
HA.com/NaturalHistory

David Herskowitz, Ext. 1610 • DavidH@HA.com

Numismatics

Coins – United States
HA.com/Coins

David Mayfield, Ext. 1277 • DavidM@HA.com
Jessica Aylmer, Ext. 1706 • JessicaA@HA.com
Win Callender, Ext. 1415 • WinC@HA.com
Chris Dykstra, Ext. 1380 • ChrisD@HA.com
Sam Foose, Ext. 1227 • SamF@HA.com
Jim Jelinski, Ext. 1257 • JimJ@HA.com
Bob Marino, Ext. 1374 • BobMarino@HA.com
Mike Sadler, Ext. 1332 • MikeS@HA.com
Beau Streicher, Ext. 1645 • BeauS@HA.com

Rare Currency
HA.com/Currency

Len Glazer, Ext. 1390 • Len@HA.com
Allen Mincho, Ext. 1327 • Allen@HA.com
Dustin Johnston, Ext. 1302 • Dustin@HA.com
Michael Moczalla, Ext. 1481 • MichaelM@HA.com
Jason Friedman, Ext. 1582 • JasonF@HA.com
Brad Ciociola, Ext. 1752 • BradC@HA.com

World & Ancient Coins
HA.com/WorldCoins

Cristiano Bierrenbach, Ext. 1661 • CrisB@HA.com
Warren Tucker, Ext. 1287 • WTucker@HA.com
David Michaels, Ext. 1606 • DMichaels@HA.com
Scott Cordry, Ext. 1369 • ScottC@HA

Sports Collectibles
HA.com/Sports

Chris Ivy, Ext. 1319 • CIvy@HA.com
Peter Calderon, Ext. 1789 • PeterC@HA.com
Derek Grady, Ext. 1975 • DerekG@HA.com
Mike Gutierrez, Ext. 1183 • MikeG@HA.com
Lee Iskowitz, Ext. 1601 • LeeI@HA.com
Mark Jordan, Ext. 1187 • MarkJ@HA.com
Chris Nerat, Ext. 1615 • ChrisN@HA.com
Jonathan Scheier, Ext. 1314 • JonathanS@HA.com

Timepieces
HA.com/Timepieces

Jim Wolf, Ext. 1659 • JWolf@HA.com

Wine
HA.com/Wine

Frank Martell, Ext. 1753 • FrankM@HA.com
Poppy Davis, Ext. 1559 • PoppyD@HA.com

Services

Appraisal Services
HA.com/Appraisals
Meredith Meuwly, Ext. 1631• MeredithM@HA.com

Corporate & Institutional Collections/Ventures
Karl Chiao, Ext. 1958 • KarlC@HA.com

Credit Department
Marti Korver, Ext. 1248 • Marti@HA.com
Eric Thomas, Ext. 1241 • EricT@HA.com

Media & Public Relations
Noah Fleisher, Ext. 1143 • NoahF@HA.com

Trusts & Estates
HA.com/Estates
Mark Prendergast, Ext. 1632 • MPrendergast@HA.com
Karl Chiao, Ext. 1958 • KarlC@HA.com

Locations

Dallas (World Headquarters)
214.528.3500 • 800.872.6467
3500 Maple Ave.
Dallas, TX 75219

Beverly Hills
310.492.8600
9478 W. Olympic Blvd.
Beverly Hills, CA 90212

New York
212.486.3500
445 Park Avenue
New York, NY 10022

DALLAS | NEW YORK | SAN FRANCISCO
BEVERLY HILLS | PARIS | GENEVA

Corporate Officers

R. Steven Ivy, Co-Chairman
James L. Halperin, Co-Chairman
Gregory J. Rohan, President
Paul Minshull, Chief Operating Officer
Todd Imhof, Executive Vice President
Kathleen Guzman, Managing Director-New York

Upcoming Auctions

U.S. Rare Coin Auctions	Location	Auction Dates	Consignment Deadline
U.S. Coin ANA	Pittsburgh	October 13-16, 2011	Closed
U.S. Rare Coins	Beverly Hills	November 7-9, 2011	Closed
U.S. Rare Coins	New York	December 7-11, 2011	October 28, 2011
F.U.N.	Orlando	January 3-8, 2012	November 25, 2011

World & Ancient Coin Auctions	Location	Auction Dates	Consignment Deadline
World Coin	New York	January 2-3, 2012	November 5, 2011
World Coin Online	Dallas	January 10, 2012	November 5, 2011

Rare Currency Auctions	Location	Auction Dates	Consignment Deadline
Currency	Orlando	January 4-9, 2012	November 19, 2011

Fine & Decorative Arts Auctions	Location	Auction Dates	Consignment Deadline
Illustration Art	New York	October 22, 2011	Closed
Modern & Contemporary Art	Dallas	October 26, 2011	Closed
Texas Art	Dallas	November 5, 2011	Closed
Art of the American West	Dallas	November 5, 2011	Closed
American & European Art	Dallas	November 8, 2011	Closed
Lalique and Art Glass	New York	November 19, 2011	Closed
Vintage & Contemporary Photography	New York	November 19, 2011	Closed
Fine Silver & Vertu	Dallas	December 7, 2011	Closed
Decorative Arts	Dallas	December 7, 2011	Closed
The Estate Auction	Dallas	February 7, 2012	December 6, 2011
Illustration Art	Beverly Hills	February 21-22, 2012	December 20, 2011
California Art	Beverly Hills	March 20, 2012	January 17, 2012
Fine Silver & Vertu	Dallas	April 10, 201	February 7, 2012
Texas Art	Dallas	May 5, 2012	March 3, 2012
Art of the American West	Dallas	May 5, 2012	March 3, 2012
American & European Art	Dallas	May 15, 2012	March 13, 2012
Vintage & Contemporary Photography	New York	May 21, 2012	March 20, 2012
Modern & Contemporary Art	Dallas	May 29, 2012	March 27, 2012
Decorative Arts	Dallas	June 11, 2012	April 9, 2012

Jewelry, Timepieces & Luxury Accessory Auctions	Location	Auction Dates	Consignment Deadline
Watches & Fine Timepieces	New York	November 18, 2011	Closed
Fine Jewelry	Dallas	December 5, 2011	Closed
Handbags & Luxury Accessories	Dallas	December 6, 2011	Closed
Fine Jewelry	New York	April 30, 2012	February 27, 2012
Handbags & Luxury Accessories	New York	May 1, 2012	February 29, 2012
Watches & Fine Timepieces	New York	May 21, 2012	March 20, 2012

Vintage Movie Posters Auctions	Location	Auction Dates	Consignment Deadline
Vintage Movie Posters	Dallas	November 18-19, 2011	Closed
Vintage Movie Posters	Beverly Hills	July 16-20, 2012	May 25, 2012

Comics Auctions	Location	Auction Dates	Consignment Deadline
Comics & Original Comic Art	Beverly Hills	November 15-17, 2011	Closed
Comics & Original Comic Art	Dallas	February 23-24, 2012	January 10, 2012

Music & Entertainment Memorabilia Auctions	Location	Auction Dates	Consignment Deadline
Vintage Guitars & Musical Instruments	Dallas	October 21-22, 2011	Closed
Music, Celebrity & Hollywood Memorabilia	Dallas	December 13-14, 2011	October 22, 2011
Vintage Guitars & Musical Instruments	Dallas	December 16-17, 2011	October 25, 2011

Historical Grand Format Auctions	Location	Auction Dates	Consignment Deadline
Militaria	Dallas	November 12, 2011	Closed
Americana & Political	Dallas	November 30, 2011	Closed
Space Exploration	Dallas	November 30, 2011	Closed
Rare Books	New York City	December 8-9, 2011	October 17, 2011
Historical Manuscripts	New York City	December 8-9, 2011	October 17, 2011
Arms & Armor	Las Vegas	January 22-23, 2012	December 1, 2011
Texana	Dallas	March 10, 2012	January 18, 2012
Art of the Americas	Dallas	Spring 2012	January 12, 2012
Americana & Political	Dallas	June 2012	April 1, 2012
Militaria	Dallas	June 2012	April 1, 2012
Space Exploration	Dallas	June 2012	April 1, 2012

Vintage Sports Collectibles Auctions	Location	Auction Dates	Consignment Deadline
Vintage Sports Collectibles	Dallas	November 10-11, 2011	Closed
Vintage Sports Collectibles	Dallas	April 26-27, 2012	March 5, 2012

Natural History Auctions	Location	Auction Dates	Consignment Deadline
Natural History	Beverly Hills	January 8, 2012	Closed

Fine & Rare Wine	Location	Auction Dates	Consignment Deadline
Fine & Rare Wine	Beverly Hills	December 1-2, 2011	October 19, 2011

HA.com/Consign • Consignment Hotline 800-872-6467 • All dates and auctions subject to change after press time. Go to HA.com for updates.

HERITAGE WEEKLY INTERNET COIN AUCTIONS • Begin and end every Sunday & Tuesday of each week at 10 PM CT.
HERITAGE MONTHLY INTERNET WORLD COIN AUCTIONS • Begin and end the second Tuesday of each month at 10 PM CT.
HERITAGE TUESDAY INTERNET CURRENCY AUCTIONS • Begin and end every Tuesday at 10 PM CT.
HERITAGE WEEKLY INTERNET COMICS AUCTIONS • Begin and end every Sunday at 10 PM CT.
HERITAGE WEEKLY INTERNET MOVIE POSTER AUCTIONS • Begin and end every Sunday at 10 PM CT.
HERITAGE WEEKLY INTERNET SPORTS AUCTIONS • Begin and end every Sunday at 10 PM CT, with extended bidding available.
HERITAGE WEEKLY INTERNET WATCH & JEWELRY AUCTIONS • Begin and end every Tuesday at 10 PM CT.
HERITAGE WEEKLY INTERNET VINTAGE GUITAR & MUSICAL INSTRUMENT AUCTIONS • Begin and end every Thursday at 10 PM CT.
HERITAGE WEEKLY INTERNET RARE BOOKS AUCTIONS • Begin and end every Thursday at 10 PM CT.
HERITAGE MONTHLY INTERNET WINE AUCTIONS • Begin and end the second Thursday of each month at 10 PM CT

9-27-2011

Auctioneers: Samuel Foose: TX 11727; CA Bond #RSB2004178; FL AU3244; GA AUNR3029; IL 441001482; NC 8373; OH 2006000048; MA 03015; PA AU005443; TN 6093; WI 2230-052; NYC 0952360; Denver 1021450; Phoenix 07006332. Robert Korver: TX 13754; CA Bond #RSB2004179; FL AU2916; GA AUNR003023; IL 441001421; MA 03014; NC 8363; OH 2006000049; NYC 1096338; Denver 1021446. Teia Baber: TX 16624; CA Bond #RSB2005525. Ed Beardsley: TX Associate 16632; NYC 1183220. Nicholas Dawes: NYC 1304724. Marsha Dixey: TX 16493. Chris Dykstra: TX 16601; FL AU4069; WI 2566-052; TN 6463; IL 441001788; CA #RSB2005738. Jeff Engelken: CA Bond #RSB2004180. Alissa Ford: CA Bond #RSB2005920. Leo Frese: CA Bond #RSB2004176; NYC 1094963. Shaunda Fry: TX 16448; FL AU3915; WI 2577-52; CA Bond #RSB2005396. Kathleen Guzman: NYC 0762165. Stewart Huckaby: TX 16590. Cindy Isennock, participating auctioneer: Baltimore Auctioneer license #AU10. Carolyn Mani: CA Bond #RSB2005661; Bob Merrill: TX 13408; MA 03022; WI 2557-052; FL AU4043; IL 441001683; CA Bond #RSB2004177. Cori Mikeals: TX 16582; CA #RSB2005645. Scott Peterson: TX 13256; NYC 1306933; IL 441001659; WI 2431-052; CA Bond #RSB2005395. Tim Rigdon: TX 16519. Michael J. Sadler: TX 16129; FL AU3795; IL 441001478; MA 03021; TN 6487; WI 2581-052; NYC 1304630; CA Bond #RSB2005412. Eric Thomas: TX 16421; PA AU005574; TN 6515. Andrea Voss: TX 16406; FL AU4034; MA 03019; WI 2576-052; CA Bond #RSB2004676; NYC #1320558. Jacob Walker: TX 16413; FL AU4031; WI 2567-052; IL 441001677; CA Bond #RSB2005394. Peter Wiggins: TX 16635. (Rev. 5-15-11)